BIG BOYS DON'T CRY

Published in 2025 by Robert W Phillips
Author © 2025 Robert W Phillips
Cover Photograph by Mabel E. Phillips
Cover & Book design by Maureen Carroll
Map created by Randy Breeden
Arial, Britanica Bold, Minion Pro, and Tahoma

Book Description: This deeply personal memoir paints a vivid picture of a bygone era, where the spirit of the American farm family shine through every challenge. Big Boys Don't Cry is more than just a coming-of-age story—it's a testament to the unbreakable bond of family and the relentless pursuit of a dream, no matter the odds.

Big Boys Don't Cry: Memoir of a Mid-Century Farm Boy / Robert W Phillips

BIO026000, BIOGRAPHY & AUTOBIOGRAPHY / Personal Memoirs
BIO006000   BIOGRAPHY & AUTOBIOGRAPHY / Historical
BIO002000   BIOGRAPHY & AUTOBIOGRAPHY / Cultural & Regional

ISBN-13: 979-8-9994297-0-4 (Paperback)

ISBN-13: 979-8-9994297-1-1   (Hardcover)

robertwphillips.com

BIG BOYS DON'T CRY

MEMOIR OF A
MID-CENTURY FARM BOY

Robert W Phillips

Dedication
To my mother, my guiding light.

Dedication
To my family
It took all of them to raise me.

Virgil Kansas • Circa 1951

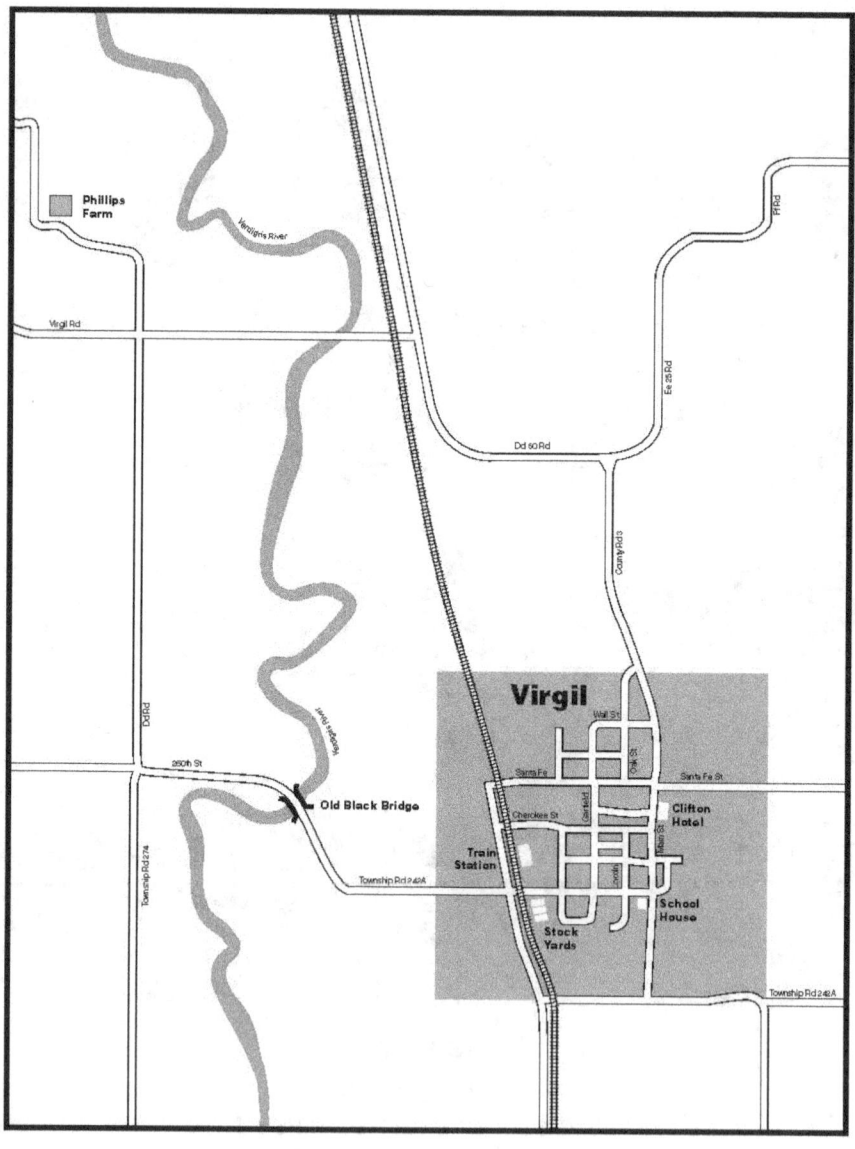

Contents

Robert W Phillips
The front cover superimposed photograph of me with Heifer was
taken by my mother Mabel E. Phillips.

INTRODUCTION

In these pages, I recount stories from my early years growing up on a one-hundred-sixty acre farm located in the beautiful Flint Hills of Kansas. My parents were tenant farmers who accepted all the uncertainties this arrangement carried with it. The events and activities of the rural community in midcentury America provide the backdrop of a simpler time when a young boy could be entertained by his dogs, cats, bottle calf, and eventually his own horse.

My family included four sisters, but only two lived at home with me as the elder two were already married. Since my sisters were all more than nine years older than I, the age disparity contributed to my being dramatically spoiled and teased. I hope the love my family had for each other comes through with every word written.

The title of my book is derived from what my mother always told me, "big boys don't cry." That was a difficult thing to learn for a youngster who was just at the age where it was easy to have tears well up in my eyes and feel like crying, especially when encountering some of life's most tragic moments. Still, like other young boys of that era, growing up strong and tough like my father was always the goal.

Even with hardships, my main focus was to become a cowboy and to have my own horse. For me "riding for the brand" was synonymous with "riding for the family." The family is everything when surviving on a little farm where it meant producing most of our own food and making a large portion of our clothes.

In 1951, we were confronted with the terrors of what was considered the worst flood ever to take place in Kansas. To see all of our crops destroyed meant no feed for livestock which then had to be sold. With no animals and no products to sell, that also meant no way to make an income. Like many other farmers devastated by losses from the flood the future looked extremely bleak.

Then another blow was dealt when we received an eviction notice from the landlord with only sixty days to relocate. But the disaster didn't stop there as my memories from long ago impart.

My *Big Boys Don't Cry* memoir is to be followed by the history of the community where I grew up titled, *The Birth and Demise of a Small Flint Hills Town*, creating a duology. This second book is to be published later this year.

It will encompass stories about the settlers arriving in Kansas for the cheap or free land after the Civil War, and how they built a thriving community with a post office, a hotel, and a newspaper. With those came oil production, arrival of the railroad, and the establishment of a very good school system which included an outstanding sports program—all to eventually regress as a declining population and now become just another forgotten "ghost town."

Chapter 1

It's a Boy!

This was the story my mother, father, and sister Frances told me about my day of birth, and my first few days after arriving home.

The weather was cold and snowy. Outside the wind was blowing and the windows on the house were rattling; the old pear tree to the south of the house was creaking and moaning as it twisted and turned in the wind. A couple of coyotes had been yipping for some time, presumably looking for companionship.

It was the wee hours of Monday morning, only one week before Christmas, and the clock had just struck midnight. Mamma let my father know that it was time to go to the hospital as she could feel I was coming. She got up and found the matches to light the kerosene lamp so they would have a little light to get ready. Mamma said it was very cold but they knew they must get started on their way. My father, after dressing and putting on his shoes said, "I will go tell the girls we are leaving." He found his way out the bedroom door but there was no light in the house except the reflection off the snow. He then went around the potbelly stove where he could still feel a little heat coming out. He then climbed up the stairs that were so steep it was almost like climbing a ladder, to the girls' room to tell them he and Mamma were leaving for Eureka.

Marilyn asked Frances, "Why are they going to Eureka?" Frances replied that their mother was going to have a baby. Marilyn did not believe her sister because she didn't even know her mother was pregnant. Marilyn, only nine years old at the time, asked "Are you sure?" Frances, 12 years old, in an excited voice said, "Yes, I am sure. Isn't this great we are going to have a baby brother or maybe a sister?"

Daddy, after telling the girls, went out and started the car to warm it up and cleaned the snow and ice off the windshield. He then went back inside and helped Mamma get her coat on while grabbing a couple of blankets off the bed, just in case they might have trouble.

They got into the car that hadn't warmed up much, and Daddy backed around so they could head out. As they pulled out of the barnyard, they could see the lights of Virgil about three miles to the southeast. No other lights could be seen because electricity had not made it to the rural areas around Virgil yet, although the snow on the ground did provide some reflection which made it not quite so dark.

Daddy could hear the tires crunching on the fresh snow and it crossed his mind that the tires on the car weren't the best. It was during World War II which had been going on for three years and had caused a shortage of tires, if you could even find any. Daddy didn't bring it up because Mamma already had a lot on her mind and was in some pain.

Daddy drove cautiously on the slick road that had a number of curves to navigate, but they took them slow. When they saw lights of an oil drilling rig in the distance, Mamma mentioned, "It sure would be nice to have some of that light to milk the cows by in the winter." It was hard to get away from thinking about farm work, even when you are going to have a baby. They soon approached the community of Hamilton, crossing the railroad tracks to reach the highway. The pavement was still a little slick during the 10 miles to reach the main route to Eureka. After that, it was only about 8 miles to go.

They had been talking the entire time, trying to keep Mamma's mind off the pain. They soon saw the Eureka Cemetery on the south side of the road and the dim lights of town, and knew they were getting close. They drove only a few blocks more to pull up in front of the Basham Hospital. What a relief to both of them!

Daddy helped Mamma out of the car and they made their way into the front entrance and inside, explaining a baby was on the way. Hurriedly they were escorted into one of the rooms where one of the nurses assured them she would get in contact with the doctor and he would be there soon. The Basham Hospital was a family-owned facility and did not have doctors there all the time, but relied on them being on call. About ten minutes later, Dr. Basham arrived.

They asked Daddy to go out into the waiting room and wait, which he did hoping everything would go okay. For Daddy, the time went by very slowly. He had never been a very patient person. He got up and paced from one end of the waiting room to the other. It felt to him hours had gone by when he finally heard a baby crying, the sound coming from the room they had taken Mamma into.

Shortly thereafter, Dr. Basham came to the waiting room and told Daddy he had a new baby boy. The doctor went on to explain to Daddy that his son had yellow jaundice and they would need to watch this condition for a few days, but it was nothing to be too concerned with. Daddy sat down and put his head in his hands saying a small prayer.

Back home, Frances and Marilyn soon got up since the excitement kept them from going back to sleep. Marilyn asked Frances again, "Are you sure they are going to the hospital for Mamma to have a baby?" Frances smiled and in a reassuring tone said, "I am sure."

There was only one heat source and it was a wood-burning, potbelly stove in the living room. Frances had watched her mother build the fire a number of times so she very carefully put smaller pieces of wood in first and then larger pieces on top of the red-hot coals from the night before. Soon there was a roaring firing and heat started coming out of the big stove. Frances stepped back and admired her fire building skills and thought what an accomplishment! For nearly 60 years she remembered the day her little brother was born and the great fire she had built, telling the story over and over again, but I never got tired of hearing it.

In the morning, Frances fixed them some cereal; she did not want to build a fire in the wood-burning cook stove that morning. They then got ready for school and waited for the school bus, looking out the kitchen window. The last thing Frances needed to do was turn the damper down with the stove almost closed. This would allow the fire to continue to burn but not very hot. The bus pulled into the barnyard and both girls went running to get on. The driver opened the door and the girls jumped on. The kids who were already on the bus greeted them with laughter and cheers as they did every morning.

Frances, in an excited voice, let everyone on the bus know she was going to have a baby brother or sister, but Marilyn remained silent. The bus pulled out and headed for Virgil. Marilyn just couldn't believe that her mother would do that to her and go and have a baby. How disappointing and embarrassing!

The family hoped it would be a boy but Daddy had also hoped for that the previous four times because he could use some help with the farm work, although the girls were excellent help in the field. They drove the horses, raked hay and drove the tractor with the hay baler. Frances was his favorite to drive the tractor while baling hay. She was therefore rewarded with a tractor umbrella to block out the hot summer sun because she had a very fair complexion. She was very proud of her tractor driving skills and very excited to get the reward of the umbrella and, of course, Daddy's words of confidence.

After I was born, Daddy returned home since he had to milk the cows and do the other chores. They named me Robert. My mother liked the name but she didn't want me called Bob or Bobbie. Freda, my oldest sister, was disappointed because she wanted to use the name Robert for her firstborn son but instead, she had three girls, so everything worked out. My sisters and I always honored our mother's wish and never let the Bob name take hold.

Since I had yellow jaundice at birth, they still worried if I would even live, so Mamma and I remained a few more days in the hospital before going home. I did get better and lived to become a healthy young boy, and now, I am considered to be an old man.

It is always fun to look at the other great things that were taking place around the world on my birthday. The other headlines of the day, December 18, 1944 were:

General MacArthur received his 5th Star.

The Germans launched a major offensive on that day which become known as the "Battle of the Bulge."

The popular songs of the day were: "Song of a Tree" sung

by Frank Sinatra, "It Could Only Be You" by Dick Haynes, and "I Am Wasting My Tears on You" by Tex Ritter.

In the *Eureka Herald,* December 21, 1944 (the first paper to come out after I was born), my birth was announced in the "Basham Hospital News" section: "Mrs. R W Phillips of Virgil was admitted Monday. A son was born the same day to Mr. and Mrs. Phillips." (Short and to the point.) No name had been given yet.

The prominent headline in the Eureka Herald of the same addition was: "Hamilton Boy was killed in action Roscoe Guffy."

My grandmother Laura Young wrote a poem upon learning of my birth. At the time, she was living at a state tuberculosis hospital just outside of Norton, Kansas where she had been for a couple of years.

"Twas a week before Christmas and much to our joy, The Angels brought to our home a dear baby boy. He has little pink fingers, and a mighty cute nose, In fact he's a darling from his head to his toes.

I wonder if Santa will bring him a toy. He must bring him something for he is our boy.

Suppose that he brings him a right pretty name for if he doesn't get one that would be a shame.

Why not call him Robert? That's a nice name and Oh I think of another one just "Little Joe."

(In reference to the name Little Joe, this is what my mother was called by her father when she was a child.)

The day I was born there were three noteworthy things that would be talked about for many years: Freda was so excited after learning she had a little brother that she drove off the road going home after teaching for the day; Frances's building of the great fire that morning; and, of course, the disappointment and embarrassment of Marilyn that her mother had a baby.

Everyone was happy when Mamma and I came home. It was the day after Christmas and all of my sisters had gathered for the homecoming. Everyone was encouraged to keep their distance as Mamma was very protective. She was well aware of the winter diseases, and since I had been born with yellow jaundice, she was even more protective.

It took a little adjustment with the girls pitching in and taking up the slack for what Mamma had been doing. They tried, but in no way could they do everything and go to school also. The main need was to separate the cream and cook for the family, which included washing the dishes. My father in later years said he would have starved to death if he had to "depend on those girls cooking all the time!" But soon, everyone settled in, and Marilyn got over her shock of a new family member and was equally happy to have a baby brother.

The most pressing problem became what clothes to put on me since they did not have any hand-me-downs from an older brother. There was, however, an abundance of little dresses. So, Mamma went to work making some trousers and little shirts, and baby nightgowns from these baby girl clothes.

Because the living room was the location of the large wood-burning stove, my crib was set there. Like any new baby with older sisters, I soon became spoiled. Even though I could not talk, I soon learned how to get the attention I wanted. I would be perfectly content when being by myself, but once someone came into the room, I would start to fuss, letting them know I was still there.

Mamma and Daddy did not take me out much in the cold weather. They wanted to make sure I was kept healthy and not exposed to the winter viruses that always go around.

Taking care of a baby was somewhat more difficult in 1944 living on a farm with no way to get hot water other than warming it on the kitchen stove, no heat other than a wood-burning potbelly stove, and no electricity. In addition, all the water had to be brought into the house hand-pumped and carried from a well about 30 yards away.

Another inconvenience was that diapers had to be washed in the outside washhouse. Water had to be heated in the kitchen and carried to the gasoline powered washing machine that included a tub and agitator, and hand-fed wringer. This also needed to be done for the rest of the family laundry which was very hard work and very uncomfortable because of no heat in the washhouse. And the worst part was hanging everything on the clothes lines. Mamma's hands would be very red, chapped and almost frozen when she came inside.

I can only imagine how hard my mother worked and the

fatigue her body must have gone through, including the stress both on her body and mind. I know she endured all of this because she had a great trust in God.

Chapter 2

I Became an Uncle

On Thursday, January 31, 1947, I became an uncle. I was only a little more than two years old when my sister Freda had a baby girl. She was named Judith Marie Gibson and born in Eureka at the Basham Hospital. Everyone was excited and happy except for Frances who complained that on the day Judy was born, she had to stay home from school with me so my mother could go meet her first grandchild.

I was so young and barely talking, and really didn't know what was going on, except this little person was taking some attention away from me. Everyone said how cute she was and that she had blonde hair like me. At first, I called her a papoose. Not sure why I called her that. Little did I know within only a few years, she would play a very important role in my life and become as close to me as a sister.

A little over a year and half later, when Judy had been walking for a little while and was just starting to say a few words, she called me Augie. I was told later by my sisters that, evidently, Judy was having a hard time saying Robert. For years we teased her about not being able to pronounce my name.

It seemed a lot of people thought I was awfully young to be an uncle but, of course, I didn't really have a lot to do with it. I guess the main thing was having a much older sister. In fact, she was 19 years older than I, and married before I was even born. It wasn't totally that rare as I have heard of people automatically becoming aunts and uncles on the day of their birth.

Chapter 3

No Angel

An incident in my life proved to my mother, father and two sisters still living at home, that I was no angel. This was not really in question at all, but where did I become under the influence of the Devil?

It was most likely in the winter of 1946 when I was only two or three years old. I had been talking for a while, but my vocabulary was not very developed yet. I actually do not remember this incident but was told about it numerous times while growing up. One thing known for sure was that it was cold outside because I was trying to put on my winter coat. In a moment of frustration trying to zip it up and after numerous tries, I uttered the words, "G**D*** it!"

Everyone in the family was standing in the kitchen, getting ready to go outside and putting on their coats when this unforgivable outburst happened. Faces all went blank, mouths dropped open and a gasp came from my mother. "Oh, my!" The angel had just lost his halo. How could this be?

Where would I have been exposed to such vile language? We did have a radio but, in those days, they didn't even use the word dang. This was also prior to me ever having friends over to play. I had been to Sunday School but it couldn't have come from there, and they all knew that it wasn't from Mamma.

Had I been questioned, I would have blamed the dogs or possibly one of the hogs. Since the only suspects were still standing in the room, not a word came from Daddy or one of the sisters as they all stood there with mouths open. As the years went by, never did a confession come forward. This is one unthinkable crime that has not been solved to this day.

If I just hadn't been so determined to zip up my coat myself, this would never have happened. It was all because I was trying to be an overachiever. I am sure it was inevitable that the time would come when I would be exposed to such language, but not so soon. Because of my desire to become a cowboy, and as I got older, I learned that the language of Roy Rogers and Dale Evans was not like the common language on those long cattle drives up the Chisholm Trail to Abilene. I guess that is why you never see a halo above any cowboy hats.

Growing up took a lot of hard work, and many times learning came from trial and error plus the imitation of what you saw and heard from other people around you. It would have been very helpful if there had been some warning labels placed around here and there.

Example: CAUTION! Words and gestures heard or seen may be found offensive. Be especially careful around other individuals near your age. It has been known there are times these individuals will try to use words and phrases that they do not have a grasp of or even an understanding, and simply are trying to impress other people or their peers with their expanded vocabulary. THIS MAY BE DANGEROUS TO YOUR HEALTH.

Chapter 4

Embarrassing

One of the most embarrassing things of my childhood oc-curred when I was three. Being afraid of the dark was a big problem of mine.

I didn't know where my parents were, but it was night and very dark outside. I told my sister Marilyn I needed to go to the toilet and do number one. She told me to just go out the backdoor and step a few feet away and go. It, being dark, there was no way I would agree to this, but she insisted. I begged her to go out with me, but she refused. Sisters were like that, only doing what was absolutely necessary. After all, I was super scared and wanted to live another day, and I knew in the dark there was a coyote just waiting for me. I probably was going to be his supper.

Finally, I had to go so badly that I stepped out onto the back porch just to see how dark it really was, and I knew I didn't want to go any farther. Then I saw a pair of my dad's knee boots by the door, the kind you slipped on your feet without shoes. The worst idea I could have ever had came to mind. I decided to go in one of the boots; they were just the right height. I then came back into the house where Marilyn was fixing something in the kitchen and she said, "See, that wasn't that bad, was it, scaredy cat?"

I went to bed thinking I had found the perfect solution to not going all the way outside. Then morning came and I got up to have breakfast when Daddy came in from milking. He looked directly at me and said, "I put my boots on this morning and found one of them was wet inside. Would you know anything about that?" At first, I said, "No" but within a few moments I had given a complete confession. Now this is something a boy never forgets and I am still embarrassed to this day, although it really was my sister's fault. She should have just taken me to the outdoor privy. That was entirely too much blame for a three-year-old to bear. Who knows what could have happened? A coyote could have gotten me; the Indian buried at the end of the drive could have scalped me; maybe the boogie man who lived in the dark could have eaten me; and oh, the list just goes on and on.

I had taken the young boy's oath: Never admit anything, except when your father has you dead to rights. Then plead for mercy with a confession...but confess only the bare minimum.

Chapter 5

R
P

Fixing My Coffee

I awoke one morning and I couldn't hear anyone in the kitchen as I always did, but there was the sound of the wind blowing outside and it was dark and cold. The old potbelly stove sitting across the room from me was roaring. I kicked off the numerous blankets as I was crawling out of bed and then went into the kitchen. I saw everyone else had eaten without awakening me and were now gone. The coffeepot sat on the stove, plus a cold pot of oatmeal which I thought didn't look too good and possibly should go in the slop bucket.

My mother always made my cup of coffee but since I had watched her a number of times, I decided I could do this. I got one of the coffee mugs and poured it about two-thirds full of coffee. Setting it down at the table, I started putting the finishing touches in it. I took the sugar bowl and put a spoon full of sugar in the coffee. Much to my surprise it did not turn white, not even a little change of color. I figured I needed to add another spoonful of sugar and still, it didn't turn color. After about ten more tries, I became very frustrated and almost in tears. This wasn't supposed to happen since I was sure I was doing everything that my mother had done when I watched her. I didn't think my sisters were playing tricks on me but I couldn't be for sure.

About that time Mamma came through the kitchen door carrying a bucket full of fresh milk. She looked at me and said, "It sure is cold out there. What have you been doing?"

Almost crying, I explained how I had tried to make my own coffee and how many spoons of sugar I had put in the cup, and it still didn't turn white! She started laughing but I felt this was no laughing matter. She poured out the cup, of what was then almost pure sugar, into the slop bucket and then poured a new cup of coffee. Setting it down, she then put in three spoonful's of sugar, and then added about one half cup of milk. Wow, it turned white like I was used to seeing! Mamma told me the milk makes it change color. I had forgotten the milk part. I guess my sisters really didn't have any part of this. I now know that was a trick I played on myself.

Chapter 6

R̵ₚ

Before Starting School

From the day I was born in 1944 and prior to my going to school in September 1950, I spent a lot of time with just my mother and father on the farm. Of course, my sisters Frances and Marilyn were around after school each day and in the summertime. But for me, there was no daycare, no going to stay with friends, and just one exception—Vacation Bible School a couple of weeks each summer.

When I was old enough to be in the yard by myself, I looked for the school bus coming toward our home, and sometimes when I was inside the house, my mother would remind me that it was about time for the bus. I think she reminded me, once in a while, a little early just to get me from under her feet in the house. "Here comes the bus," I would yell, and then I and the dogs would go charging off to where the bus let my sisters exit. I was always so happy to see them. I am not sure they felt the same about me. I loved looking through their lunch pails to see if they maybe had left something. These leftovers tasted so good. Sometimes the dogs thought they should get some, but I usually had other ideas. A young boy is always hungry.

Thinking back, I probably spent the most time during these years with my mother; my father would have been outside working around the farm. One of his big jobs during the winter was cutting firewood for the potbelly stove and, before that, the wood-burning cook stove. He would go to the timber, a very exciting place for exploring, to find the trees that had already fallen, trim them with the ax, and cut them up with the buzz saw. This was a saw mounted to the front of his tractor. It had a very large circular blade that created a tremendous amount of noise when it was started. It made the birds fly away all at the same time, creating a lot of noise with their flapping wings, and then more noise when a log was being cut. I was never allowed to go to the timber except when Mamma came along. She considered it unsafe otherwise. She even worried about Daddy and his safety. Saw blades turning and trees falling could present a lot of opportunity for an accident.

It was amazing what a boy could find exploring around the trees on the hillside. The ground there was covered with lots of leaves, acorns, walnuts, some even cracked by the squirrels and rocks sticking out of the ground. There were also birds of every color and shape, big and little rabbits, and sometimes one of our barn cats now and then. I guess they were looking for a mouse to eat.

One time I even found where a previous tenant had dumped some junk. There was very little there—some strange shaped bottles and part of a wooden crate. I wondered why they didn't burn it in their stove. We wouldn't have been that wasteful.

But again, the timber was considered off limits to me when Daddy was cutting wood. And when he wasn't there, I was too scared to go in by myself anyway.

Exploring was about the most exciting thing a young boy could do. It didn't have to be in the timber; it could be almost anywhere you hadn't been before. Exploring was how you would find the new litter of kittens or maybe a box turtle, baby rabbits, baby birds in a nest, strange bugs, special rocks, and of course, snipes…if you believed your sisters. This last one I never found so I still question my sisters' creditability. I think they considered me less than smart and, in fairness, I gave them a number of reasons to doubt my intelligence. I can't remember one such instance right now, but give me a couple of weeks.

Time with my father

I didn't think there was anything more fun than being with my father. He was a big man who always wore bib overalls and some type of hat which was usually a straw hat in the summer, and in the winter a cap that had flaps he could pull down over his ears. It seemed that he also wore knee-boots most of the time. He would stand so stately with his hands holding onto the shoulder straps of his overalls, feet spread apart, head tilted back with his straw hat on, and then that big smile watching me lead my calf around.

He also chewed tobacco. I think my mother wished he would quit that habit, but she never said much about it. He never quit until many years later.

My father always seemed to have a glow on his face when we were doing things together, plus he radiated a feeling of love and pride. He usually referred to me as "son" which gave me a warm feeling inside.

When it was too cold or Daddy was doing something that I couldn't be with him, I was with my mother, which was most of the time. We would either be in the house or going places she needed to go. Sometimes we would go down to the train depot to leave the cream can and pick up an empty one. One time I remember going into the Clifton Hotel. That place was extremely scary. Mamma and I walked up to the counter and an older woman came to ask what we wanted. I totally hid behind my mother's dress and coat. I mean, that woman looked scary! I don't know who she was but I was afraid and tried to avoid going into the Clifton in the future.

It was usually a lot of fun to go into the Commons' Store because Mrs. Commons was so friendly to Mamma and me. In most cases, Mamma would buy me a piece of penny candy. I would tell my sisters about getting the candy and I think it made them jealous, or maybe not.

Every once in a while, we would stop at the post office to buy some stamps. Most of these things we did in the winter since Mamma was too busy in the spring and summer, getting ready for winter.

Being in the house during the cold or rainy days was bad for me, but I believe it may have been worse for Mamma. She would say, "I can't wait until your sisters get home so they can put your snow suit on and take you outside."

Chapter 7

The Farm

My family moved to our new farm near Virgil, Kansas on March 1, 1944 before I was born in December that year. The previous two years they had been living just southeast of Madison operating a small dairy, milking cows and making home deliveries to residents of Madison and selling milk directly to grocery stores. Those were the days before the health laws requiring milk to be pasteurized before selling to the public.

Previously the decision to move to Madison was brought on by World War II. They did not want to move from the Virgil area, but the farm they were living on was owned by the Storrer family. They had a son, Reldon, who was a senior in high school and would be eligible for the draft upon graduation. He needed a farm of his own to obtain the farm deferment, so my folks were asked to vacate. This, as you might think, absolutely did not cause a strain on the relationship between our two families. My father and mother had been great friends with the Storrers as soon as they moved to the Virgil area in October 1929. They understood Reldon should have the farm.

The farm near Madison was not very big but it did allow them to set up a dairy. They had electricity and running water which was the first time they had ever lived with such luxuries. But with a small operation, they were barely able to financially survive.

Prior to moving to Madison in 1942, all of my sisters had been born. Freda was 15, Lola was 14, Frances was 9 and Marilyn was 6. They all were enrolled in the Madison School District. Freda and Lola graduated in May 1944 after staying with another family for two months so that they could graduate from Madison when the rest of the family moved back to Virgil. They graduated the same year because Lola completed two years in one. We considered her the brightest apple on the tree.

Up until this time, my family had only farmed with horses. The landlord Martha Bays, who owned the new Virgil farm, required my dad to have a tractor as a tenant farmer. He purchased a used Allis-Chalmers to satisfy this requirement.

The farm was approximately 160 acres. With about 100 acres of actual farmland in the rich Verdigris River Valley, it also included 30 acres of timber and the remaining 30 acres pasture and barnyard. It was here that the family lived when I was born.

The Little Two-Story House On The Prairie

We lived in a small two-story house located on top of a hill just at the edge of the Flint Hills that overlooked the beautiful and fertile Verdigris River Valley. The few acres of hardwood timber grew on the hillside leading down to the floodplain, thus dividing the grassland from the fertile soil in the valley with frontage on the Verdigris River. This would have been the perfect farm for those early settlers looking for fertile soil, timber and water. It was still the perfect place for us.

The view in all directions was excellent. You could see the sunrise coming up over the hills on the east side of the valley. On most early mornings before you could see the sun, there would be a very soft yellow or pink to light-red glow. Then the bright sunrays came shooting across the sky as the sun would rise just a little more.

To the west there were almost always beautiful sunsets settling over the Flint Hills with hundreds of different sky colors accented with cloud formations and rolling hills. Sometimes during the summer, you would see large cumulus clouds soaring to heights of thousands of feet with the sun shining on them to create beautiful shades of white, gray, black, silver and a touch of gold now and then. Constantly moving clouds might suddenly produce a bright beam of golden sunlight, shooting to the earth from an opening in their formations.

Then looking to the southeast, you could see the beautiful little village of Virgil sitting on the hill. The three-story brick school house, with its large bell tower on top, looked so stately. At night you could see the soft electric light glowing from the village homes along with a few street lamps. What a setting!

Looking back, the ironic thing I find in life is that you don't know or appreciate what you have until it's gone. I know this is the case with me and our Virgil home, and especially my family, neighbors, friends and classmates.

The house was painted white but most of the paint had either faded away or chipped off. It seemed that we had an adequate number of windows with screens to provide cross ventilation, helping the house to keep somewhat cool at night during those very hot summer months.

There were three doors to enter but only one was ever used as far as I recall. We had a door on the west side of the house with a very small porch, which I assume was supposed to be the front door. Out by the road there was a gate but no path leading from the front door to the road, just weeds and prairie grass. We did not have a lawnmower as we let mother nature take care of that. Besides, we always had furniture sitting in front of the door. I was told this door was for the really important people to enter like the preacher, the peddler, the banker and the governor. Although, when the peddler came, he entered through the back door. The rest of those mentioned actually never came to our house, so the front door was never needed.

One of the other doors was on the north side of the house and was never used. It opened into the kitchen, had no screen on it or any step to the outside, however, it did have a glass window which allowed more light into the house.

The third door was the one used. It was on the south side of the house and opened onto a small screened-in porch. This porch was where the cream separator was located, and the area where boots were taken off and stored along with outside work coats and, of course, the five-gallon slop bucket for the hogs.

Moving inside, the kitchen also served as the dining room. This was really where most of the family activity took place. In the early days when we lived there, my mother cooked on a wood-burning stove, and later a fuel oil stove, and then one that operated on propane.

The living room is where I slept on a daybed. The main heat for the house was a large wood-burning potbelly stove that was also in this room. The stove could really put off the heat. On oc-casion, with the right kind of wood, particularly Osage Orange or more commonly called a hedge tree, the old stove would start glowing a bright red at the base of the fire box. At this point it almost became scary; a fear of starting the house on fire concerned everyone. The other things in the living room were the family's radio, Mamma's sewing machine, a couple of rocking chairs and a piece of furniture used as a desk.

This was the same radio that the whole family gathered around on December 8, 1941 to hear Franklin D. Roosevelt give his passionate speech about the Japanese bombing of Pearl Harbor. That was the day many things turned the world upside down and caused horrendous things to happen, includ-ing the family having to move to Madison as mentioned in an earlier chapter.

Also in the house were two small bedrooms on the first floor: one for my parents and the other used for storage which also sometimes became the sick room if a family member was ill. I can remember using this room myself, especially when I had the measles. Oh, how any light coming in would make my eyes hurt so much! My mother had to put blankets over the one win-dow to block all light from coming in. I remember waking up one morning and my eyes were so matted over they would not open. I thought I had lost my vision; it was a scary moment.

Upstairs was just one big unfinished room which my sisters used as their bedroom. The stairs going up were very steep, almost like climbing a ladder. The only heat to this room came from the brick chimney radiating warmth from the potbelly stove below, and it wasn't a lot. Fortunately, there were three win-dows which did provide some ventilation in the summer.

The walls were covered with an ugly, flimsy material with no insulation. It was so cold that my sisters put heated bricks into their beds before getting into bed just to get a little heat started before their body heat could take over. I hardly ever went up there because the room was so cold. It was almost like sleep-ing outside, especially when it snowed. My sisters would some-times wake up in the morning and snow would have blown in through cracks around the windows and cover their beds.

This house was my family's home for almost eight years.

Being a house for tenant farm families, it never got much attention. My mother and sisters did put up another layer of wallpaper once. We never expected anything better while living there although we did get electricity around 1950. I am not sure who paid for this improvement, but I think the landlord did so reluctantly.

Recycling and Conservation

Life on the farm meant recycling and conservation. For instance, the slop bucket was our garbage disposal. Talk about recycling and great care of the environment, we did it! Most things were used over and over and we never used a plastic straw.

Back then, we went to great extremes to use things until they were used up or worn out. One of the most extreme was probably in the outhouse and using the Montgomery Ward catalog as toilet paper. What few paper sacks that were brought home from the store, were used for carrying lunches and giving items from the garden to the neighbors.

We hardly ever bought anything in tin cans, and when we did, they could not only be used as a container for fishing worms, they could be cut apart and the metal used to close holes in the floor so mice could not get in the house. These small pieces of tin could even be used to patch holes in the wooden wagon boxes.

We always grew our own potatoes and there was no need for a plastic bag. If I was lucky and we had the money, Mamma would buy a few bottles of pop, strawberry being my favorite. The bottles could be returned for two cents each. Then as I got older, picking up pop bottles along the roadside was a good way to make a little money, thus helping the environment as we now know. There were many other such instances. The carriers for six bottles of pop were sometimes made of metal and could be used over and over. Then there were the wooden bottle carriers that would hold a whole case of twenty-four.

We always had our milk from the cows but for those city folks who needed to buy milk at the store, the milk was put into glass bottles to be used over and over. The only thing not reused was the round cardboard put on top of the bottle to keep the milk in the bottle.

When Mamma bought flour (it was always in cloth bags), she used the cloth to make tea towels and aprons. Once in a while she would even make clothes for my sisters. I'm not sure they liked going to school dressed as a flower sack. In the summer, my mother bought a bushel of peaches for canning. That bushel basket, after emptied, really went to some good uses and the home-canned peaches were wonderful.

Livestock feed from the feed store came in gunnysacks, but more properly referred to as burlap bags. There were a million uses for these sacks around the farm. I remember my father using them even for fighting grass fires. He first dunked them in the water tank and then went about beating out the fire with the wet sack.

Another act of conserving resources was what my sisters did. At night they took their gum out of their mouths and put it on the bed headboard, then in the morning retrieve it and continue chewing.

I am sure I could give many examples of how we reused things, but my point is that we weren't wasteful. You could definitely say we were friendly to the environment. I really don't want anyone to blame my generation for the problems we now have with too much trash. Not only did we love our neighbors, we loved mother nature and acted like it.

As aforementioned, the kitchen was always where most of the activity took place. It was where the family sat and talked after meals, especially supper, and where all of the vegetable canning took place, consuming numerous hours each year. The butter was also churned in this room, another time-consuming task. When someone stopped by, they would sit down at the kitchen table to visit.

In the kitchen there was always a tea kettle on the stove, a dishpan to do dishes, and a bucket of water with a dipper to either take a drink from or to pour into something for cooking. There was also a Hoosier cabinet which was a place where flour and sugar was stored, and it included a porcelain countertop that could be pulled out for working with food, or rolling out pie crusts. In addition, there were storage spaces for pots, pans, and bowls. We did not have the type of cabinets as there are today, but instead used what we call hutches where we kept dishes and more kitchen items.

Just about thirty feet to the east of the house was a small building sitting on a small hill that was created by the root cellar underneath. The building, measuring approximately 10 by 14 feet, was the washhouse. Not too far to the east of this building was a well with a hand pump where all the water for the house and washing came from. It is hard to envision today all the effort that was needed to obtain water for daily usage. Since there were no electric pumps, the hand pump was also used to provide all the water for the livestock that was kept in the barnyard including chickens, hogs, cows and horses. Out in the pasture, their water came from a pond. In the winter, the ice had to be chopped to make a hole so the livestock could drink.

The root cellar also served as a storm shelter, although I do not remember ever going there in the threat of a tornado. The root cellar was most times referred to as just the cellar. This was used as storage for a large portion of the winter's food. This included potatoes, onions, canned vegetables such as green beans, tomatoes, corn, beets, carrots, peas, kraut and many types of pickles. The large bin of potatoes had a wire screen bottom to allow air to circulate through them so they would not spoil. Then there were the many bunches of onions hung for drying.

My sisters told me of the great satisfaction our mother would get each fall, standing there looking at the hundreds of jars in perfect rows filled with colorful vegetables ready for winter. These jars represented a tremendous number of hours of work, from preparing the seedbeds to planting the seeds in the early spring, then the weeding and harvesting throughout the summer. There was also the stress of insects and weather in the garden. Most of the time we had very abundant gardens, but there was always the worry about having enough rain and not too much wind.

The first items planted were what is called the cool season plants such as radishes, onions, lettuce, carrots, cabbages, and then cantaloupe, watermelon and cucumber. Next, after the threat of frost was over, tomato plants would be set out. In addition, there were the beds of perennial plants such as asparagus and strawberries.

What must not be forgotten was Mamma's zinnias, usually two rows which added color to the garden. I do not remember Mamma ever cutting any of these flowers to bring inside the house. Each year she would collect the seeds and keep them for the next year's planting. The other flowers in the yard consisted of irises, planted most likely years earlier which kept multiplying over the years. They needed attention, which they never got, but still provided lots of color in the spring. There was also a trumpet vine growing up and around the back screen door with beautiful orange-colored flowers. Then about twenty-five feet from the backdoor was a big overgrown lilac bush and the lone old pear tree which would bloom early in the spring with the most beautiful white flowers. The tree produced hundreds of pears that were made into preserves. I often ate a number of them too early in the season and got a stomach ache.

Later came the preparation of the vegetables for canning. First was harvesting everything and then preparing them such as snapping the green beans to shelling the peas, and cutting the sweet corn off of the cobbs. All the jars had to be cleaned and sanitized before anything could be put in them and then the actual canning process used hot water baths and a pressure cooker. It had to be done to perfection to prevent poisoning from improper handling. Mamma was very particular in this part of the process.

Oh, how hot the house became on those numerous days of canning! My mother always looked totally exhausted at the end of each day and I am sure she was. She often said, "There is always a cool week in August." This is something my sisters and I would look forward to every summer. I don't remember any August where there was not. When the cool week came, we would pronounce, "This must be Mamma's cool week in August."

In later years when we all lived apart and the cool week came, we telephoned each other, remembering how our mother looked forward to that cool break and all of our thoughts would go to her—a wonderful, thoughtful, loving, extremely hard-working mother. Even today, when August comes, I look for the cool week, and when it arrives, I pronounce to my wife and kids, "This is Mamma's cool week in August." Oh, how we loved her!

Just think of having to plan your grocery list for a whole year and then buying it in the form of seeds. My sisters told me how my mother spent countless hours reading the seed catalogs which would come in the mail in the fall of each year. She seemed to get great pleasure out of this in planning the food we would eat. Regrettably, the end products did not turn out to be as beautiful and productive as the catalogs said they would, although they were very close sometimes.

Garden

The garden was made ready by first covering it with the spreading of chicken manure from the chicken house late each fall, and a little more manure from the cow lot by the milk barn. Then in late winter, when the ground wasn't frozen, my father would plow it. He first used a walking plow pulled by one horse, and then later used the tractor and plow.

One nice and warm day, Daddy was plowing and I was following along walking with my bare feet in the furrow. This felt so good with the ground so soft and cool. Then the unexpected happened when the plow turned-up a board with a nail in it. Unfortunately, I stepped on it, puncturing my foot and causing my blood to run. The pain was excruciating. The nail was very rusty as it appeared to have been there a number of years.

My mother took me into the house and washed it the best she could. She took a wad of my father's chewing tobacco and placed it on the wound with me holding it. I'm not really sure what the tobacco was supposed to do, but it must have done the job. I survived even without a tetanus shot which would be unthinkable today.

The Chicken Houses

We had two chicken houses: one for raising baby chicks and one for the hens to roost (commonly referred to as sleeping) with special boxes where the hens could nest and lay eggs.

In the winter my mother would receive two or three catalogs

from the different hatcheries and, after much study and figuring, she placed an order. She purchased chickens both for producing eggs and eating. They were delivered by the rural mail carrier who normally left the mail at the mailbox by the road but, on these days, he brought the chickens up to the house. My mother would be expecting them.

It was an exciting day. There would be three or four large boxes with holes in them and the constant sound of chirping baby chicks. As soon as they arrived, they were brought into the house so they would not get too cold. I understand that even today the post office might deliver baby chicks.

All of these little chicks entered the brooder house which was relatively small for the number of chicks, but was kept warm with a special heater that ran on kerosene. Raising the chicks was primarily my mother's job and she would especially want everyone to stay out of her way. I would have loved to get down on the ground and hold those very cute little balls of soft feathers that were running all over constantly squawking "cheap, cheap."

We always seemed to have lots of chickens but I'm not sure of the number. First, we had laying hens which provided us with lots of eggs, and I do mean lots. I should say lots of eggs in the summertime. In the winter they slowed down.

Then there were the pullets for eating, mostly frying. These are the ones we referred to as spring chickens, young and tender. In our family we ate many fried chickens. I think we ate fried chicken every day after they got big enough to butcher until they were gone, which was in the fall. Each family member had their favorite piece(s). Mine were the legs and gizzard, my father's was the liver, and my mother's was the neck. I think she knew no one else liked it and she didn't want it to go to waste. When the chickens were first big enough to eat, my mother even cooked the feet. I found this a little strange, but if Mamma cooked it, it was good enough to eat. There really wasn't much meat on the feet, maybe just gristle rolled in flour, but today I just think it was strange.

Preparing a frying chicken was not an easy process. First you had to catch the dang thing, then remove its head either by chopping it off or just wring it off with your hand. I helped with the chopping sometimes but never wringed its head off. This was my mother's specialty, and then she let the body flop around for a few minutes like it was still alive.

The next step was removal of the feathers. This was done by holding the chicken by its legs and dunking it into a scalding bucket of water. Just preparing the scalding water was a process by itself. A bucket of water had to be retrieved from the well, put on the stove until it boiled, and then taken outside to where the chopping block was now set up to pluck the feathers.

After dunking the chicken, it was time to pull the feathers out, which was relatively easy, just time consuming. I got to help with this step but never did a very good job as my mother always had to go back and finish what I had missed. The feathers that were unable to be pulled out, had to be singed off over an open flame, usually using the kitchen stove. This created a very repulsive odor.

Then came the most undesirable part—taking the intestines out and finding the gizzard, liver, and heart. The chicken could then be cut apart to soak in a salt water bath until it was cooked a short time afterwards.

Until we got our propane powered refrigerator around 1948, we had no way to keep food cool and from spoiling. The hogs got a lot of leftovers that could have been preserved if we had refrigeration. Hogs will eat anything. I mean anything. I think they would eat a little boy if given the chance.

This is just one example of how hard it was to be a farm wife and mother in the late 40's and early 50's. This was especially true with no electricity, no running water, no indoor plumbing, no hot water tank, and when it came to baking, no electric mixer.

Laundry

Another example of the difficulty during that time was the laundry. My mother was extremely concerned about how clean we were, and especially me being the little boy of the family. I just didn't understand how all that dirt got on my pants and shirt. I knew for sure I hadn't gotten that way by just walking the dogs to the barn. Of course, one always had to pet them and help them chase a rabbit that might have suddenly appeared and was running away, ending up in a woodpile where maybe two or three pieces of wood might need to be removed to reach it.

I can remember my Mamma asking, "How did your knees get so dirty? You only put those pants on less than ten minutes ago."

"Mamma, I can't help it that the rabbit ran into the woodpile and the dogs needed some help."

I am sure that being a boy, following four sisters, I was at a big disadvantage. After all, what did girls know about all the things a little boy has to do?

Prior to my being born, my mother washed everything in an old fashioned, primitive, hand-powered washing machine. My sisters told me that one day a peddler stopped at our place and showed my mother and father a washing machine that had an agitator, ringer, a hose to drain the water, and was powered by a small gasoline motor with a very long exhaust pipe, somewhere around twenty feet.

The salesman, being extremely smart, said he would leave it for a couple of weeks and when he came back, they could let him know if they wanted it. The machine worked well and helped my mother tremendously, so even though it was a lot of money for the time, my father said, "We will keep it." So now on wash days, there was always heard the "putt, putt, putt" of the motor.

The washing machine had to be such a blessing and time-saver. And even though they didn't know it at the time they bought it, it later proved to be such a lifesaver when I was born. No one had to carry the used water from the wash house, but just put a hose on the machine and simply let it run out onto the ground outside. Still, I can't imagine how hard it was to do diapers when they didn't even have disposables then.

Drying The Laundry

This was another task which consumed a lot of time because you were at the mercy of the weather. The wet laundry was hung on a clothesline by wooden pins to dry in the open air. The one big plus was that the clothes smelled so good and fresh. But if it was raining, you normally would try to wait a day or two if necessary. If she couldn't wait, my mother hung clothes all over the inside of the house. Cold weather was another obstacle because, even if it was freezing, the laundry had to be hung outside to dry. This was an extremely harsh job and Mamma's hands would turn red and become very inflamed and hurt. The clothes even sometimes froze and, when you took them down, they were stiff as a board.

Ironing

My mother was very particular about how her family looked, even though a lot of our clothes were very worn and home-made in most cases. This meant everything we wore had to be ironed and clean. Fortunately, my mother had pant stretchers to keep the wrinkles out of my father's pants and overalls. But for all else, ironing was another tedious job that had to be done.

Sisters

As my sisters got older, they were able to do many of the jobs around the house to help out. Freda, Lola and Frances also helped in the field with my father, either driving the horses or tractor. Freda told her daughter Judy in later years, the reason she was such a bad cook was because she was always outside working with our father and didn't have the chance to learn that skill.

Farmers With Milk Cows Never Get A Day Off

Farmers and farm families knew they had to work seven days a week even though they did not put as many hours in on Sundays. There were things that simply had to be done.

First was the milking. If the cows were not milked every day, they would soon stop giving milk until they had another calf. This was commonly referred to as a cow going dry. Our family depended on milk and cream production for both food and income. Then in the winter, all animals needed to be fed and watered, but in the summer some of the livestock could get by with grass in the pasture and water was available in the ponds.

The chores were so important to my father that before we would leave to go somewhere, he would say: "We got to hurry up and get going so we can get started back." And almost as soon as we got anywhere, he would start worrying about getting ready to go back home. Maybe this is why we never went many places or far from home.

Milk House

Our milk house was pretty sad. The roof sagged and leaked, and the walls were not tight, allowing some wind to blow in. The doors hung crooked on their hinges, and the floor was just dirt which would get somewhat muddy if there was much rain or snow. It was big enough to bring in four cows to milk at a time, which was what we had. The barn had no lights so in the fall and winter, a kerosene lantern was hung on the rafter above the cow being milked.

The fun part was the barn cats. They were not pets but simply there to get rid of the mice that were very plentiful. Every milking, my mother or father would squirt a stream of milk from the cow's teat into a cat's mouth. To get a really good drink, they had to stand on their hind legs while trying to get the perfect position. It was fun to tease them. After the milking was finished, my parents poured a little milk into a pan for them. That was all they got fed from us. The rest of their diet consisted of the mice, bugs and other creatures they caught in the barn or the timber behind the barn.

Even though all this might sound pretty gloomy to some, no one seemed to complain; it was just life on the farm. Our neighbors were going through the same things and my grandparents had lived pretty much the same way. We never went to bed hungry; we just went there tired.

We were proud to be farmers. After I moved to town later in my life, one of my farm friends, Larry Driskill, very much insulted me by calling me a "city slicker." Oh, what a low blow! Call me anything but don't call me a city slicker. I would rather have had cow manure on my pants than soft dishwater hands. I just wanted to be a cowboy or at least a country kid.

The Big Barn

This was where the hay was stored and the horse stalls were located. The hay, mostly alfalfa, had lots of nutrients and was wonderful feed for the livestock. The hay bales were taken from the field on wagons to the barn. Getting the hay up to the loft was done by using a pulley hung in the center of the barn, and running a rope up to the pulley and back down to the hay wagon. The end of the rope was connected to a hook put into the hay bale and the other end was connected to a horse. The horse was then led out from the barn, and the hay bale would go upward. This was very labor-intensive since you needed someone to lead the horse and hook the bale, and then walk the horse out, thus raising the hay bale.

Corn Crib

This was a different kind of building. It had a roof to keep rain and snow out. The floor was wooden with walls made of wooden boards that ran around the sides with about two-inch openings in between to let air circulate in and out of the corn.

There were also a couple of doors on the east side so corn could be shoveled in from the wagon when bringing the ear corn from the field.

The Hog Pen

The hog pen was the most disgusting place on the farm. I have now in later years heard of people who make pigs their pets. I can't even imagine that!

Our hogs only did a few things. One was lying around sleeping and if they could, they would sleep in a big mud hole filled with the most disgusting brown smelly water. Another thing was routing in their pen. They would take their nose (which I believe was designed for digging) and dig. They even dug so much around the fences that they could get out. Once a hog dug out, it was a big problem. You had to catch it plus all of his friends who got out with him, put them back in the pen, and fix the fence.

Another thing about hogs was how much they loved to eat. I mean really loved to eat. At feeding time, they got so excited they went completely crazy, running and jumping over each other. And then there was the squealing. My, how they would squeal!

Then they fought. They acted as if they had never been fed before and had been deprived of food, biting and again jumping over each other.

Outhouse

The outhouse was pretty disgusting although the hog pen may have edged it out. This little building was where we went to relieve ourselves and it usually smelled rather bad. It had two places for people to sit, but I never knew of two people going in there at the same time. Also, sitting on the bench with the two holes was, in most cases, an out-of-date Montgomery Wards catalog. They were great to look at and, when you were finished, you could tear out a page or two to clean yourself off. Welcome to our farm.

Chapter 8

My Animals

Animals played a huge part in my young life. Our family had two dogs when I was born—Old Shep and Tubsey.

When I was very young, my sister Lola and her husband Bill gave me a totally black cocker spaniel puppy which I got to name. She was very rambunctious, jumping up and knocking me over, attacking me with lots of licking, and following me everywhere. What a buddy!

When asked if I had a name for her, it was easy. "I'll call her Happy." It was so great to have her follow me around. My mother always knew that wherever the dogs were, I could be found. All three dogs usually were together but Old Shep was much slower than the other two because of his age. When I wasn't outside, the dogs would lie around the back porch waiting for something to happen or maybe me to come outside. They barked at any car that pulled into the barnyard, announcing the visitor's arrival, which didn't happen often.

The dogs never came inside the house. It was just a rule that everyone knew, and the dogs understood it well. The cats stayed in both barns; they knew their place. I only played with the kittens when they were very young and still nursing.

The dogs and cats hated each other and I am sure we didn't do anything to encourage them getting along. I remember when I was older, I saw a dog and cat together. I thought this was a freak of nature. Dogs and cats were not meant to be friends. This dislike of each other was as natural as the sun coming up each morning.

Whenever you saw a cat, it was likely for you to encourage the dog to chase the cat by saying, "sick em," although you knew the cat would always get away. You didn't want the cat hurt; it was just the chase that was exciting.

Then at the age of four, I got a baby calf. My father would let me bottle feed it sometimes and he made a rope halter so I could lead her around the barnyard. We were great friends and I loved this little calf. I just called her Heifer. It was not common on farms for us to name our meals but I never looked at Heifer as a meal.

We would go see Mamma at the washhouse or maybe at the clothesline if she was there. One place we did not go was the garden. Heifer was just too careless where she walked and Mamma became somewhat unhappy if we stepped on the plants, especially the strawberries. Whenever we found Mamma, she was always very happy and I could see the love in her eyes matched her smile.

After Mamma petted Heifer, we were usually off to check the hogs. Heifer was always a little scared of them and oh how the pigpen smelled bad! As we got close to the pigs, they got really excited, probably thinking we were bringing food which I often did. On the way to see them, we stopped by the corncrib to get a couple ears of corn. They became really excited when I threw the ears into their pen. They would squeal and jump around in the mud, biting each other and acting really crazy. The splashing around made the pigpen muddier and the hogs spread that mud everywhere. And it smelled!

Heifer sometimes tried to get away from them and then start a bucking fit herself. I would just stand there and laugh, holding on to her lead rope.

Once in a while, when the pigpen was really muddy, it splashed like water. If I was too close to the fence, I'd come away wearing the mud, accompanied with worst smell imaginable.

When I finally got up the nerve, I would go into the house and Mamma would say in an unhappy voice, "What have you been in?" or maybe, "Have you been in the pigpen?" No little boy would ever get in the pigpen because they might eat him. To make it worse was, if you did get into the mud bath, say on a Monday, it was a long time to the Saturday bath.

My mother wouldn't make me wait until Saturday in those cases, but being given a bath with an old rag in the wash pan wasn't a pleasant experience—standing in the kitchen, half naked while Mamma scrubbed me without mercy. I was sure she didn't have to rub quite so hard, but worst of all was when a sister would walk in and start laughing. That was very cruel.

I even had a few young fryer chickens as pets. We had gotten them to raise and sell for me to make money to get a horse someday. The only problem was when many of them would try to eat the worms off the fishing poles which I had not properly stored. They swallowed the worm and the hook, and then died.

A few of these chickens did live and Mamma sold them for one dollar a piece. Maybe we sold as many as fifteen. I don't remember for sure, but later I still did get my horse. What a lucky cowboy I was!

Chapter 9

Rɸ

Teasing

My sisters, who lived at home, played tricks on me. I had four sisters and that was good most of the time, but sometimes I had my doubts.

My two older sisters were married to tenant farmers, and the other two eventually became teachers who taught in small one-room country schools. They were following in my mother's footsteps as she had also taught in a one-room country school in the southeastern part of Greenwood County in Ward District.

The married sisters weren't the problem. I believe my two younger sisters felt they had a duty to ensure that I was tortured with their tricks. In return, I felt obligated to get even whenever possible, which meant I must lie in wait for the perfect opportunity.

The first trick occurred when I was about four years old and very gullible. My sisters Frances and Marilyn proposed a snipe hunt. It was one of those wonderful, almost perfect spring days—the smell of spring flowers in the air, the warmth of the bright sun, cool breeze, the sounds of crows soaring overhead, and robins singing in trees. I wondered why every day couldn't be like this one. And to make it really special, my sisters wanted to spend some time with me. I should have known something was up.

My sister Marilyn went to the feed room in the barn to get a burlap sack and brought it out to where Frances and I were waiting by the path to the pigpens. This was also one of the ways we could go to reach the area with a large group of trees. Frances smiled and said, "We are going snipe hunting."

I loved the timber area because it was like exploring in the jungle. There were always a lot of squirrels, a few rabbits and, now and then, a box turtle or two. Since there were walnut trees, there was an abundance of walnuts which had fallen to the ground the year before. I just knew this was going to be fun because being out in nature was my thing.

We came to what my sisters thought was the perfect place to catch some snipes. I looked around and we had gone so far that we could not see the house or barn. About this time, I asked, "What does a snipe look like?" They both replied almost simultaneously, but did not give the same description. Frances said, "They are small like a rabbit." And Marilyn laughing said, "They are white with big ears and red spots on them." I knew I had never seen anything like this before, but my big sisters knew a lot, and I was sure of that.

Frances then started to explain how this was going to work. She and Marilyn were going to go down the hill and drive the snipes through the two trees we were standing by, and all I had to do was catch them and put them in the bag. It was at this time I became a little concerned. This meant I was going to be left alone, and I wasn't too comfortable with that.

I waited there until they got out of sight and I took off as fast as a scared little boy can go. I ran all the way back to the house without stopping or looking back. When I crashed through the screen door going into the house, Mamma said, "Where are your sisters?" I, breathing hard replied, "They left me in the timber and I came home!" Chuckling, she mused, "Oh, I see." Soon both sisters came in laughing. Marilyn continued the ruse. "We drove all those snipes up to where you were, but when we got there, you were gone and we found the bag halfway between the timber and here. Why did you leave?"

I replied, "Because I figured out you were playing a trick on me and doubted you were telling me the truth." I just didn't understand why my sisters thought it was so much fun to tease me. After all, there were two of them and just one of me.

Trick number two was: How to see stars during the daytime. A few months after the snipe hunt, we all finished breakfast, but remained sitting at the table just talking. It was so cold no one was in a hurry to get back outside, even me. We had pancakes for breakfast that morning, and I had my cup of coffee with lots of cream and sugar. Frances suddenly turned to me and said, "Robert, do you know you can see the stars during daylight?"

"No, I didn't know you could," I answered.

"Would you like us to show you?" Marilyn asked. And, of course I said, "Sure!"

Marilyn then continued, "Get me one of Daddy's old coats and we will show you."

Being very young and not really trusting of my sisters now, I wondered what must they be up to, but I wanted to see the stars. I handed one of Daddy's old coats to Marilyn and she said, "You will need to lie down on these two chairs I have put together and look up."

I asked, "Am I going to see stars from inside the house? How can that be without even seeing the sky?"

Marilyn said to me, "You will see." She then pointed to the coat to cover me and told Daddy, "I need you to hold this end right here, and Frances, you will need to hold this end here."

Now I am lying down looking up, certain this wasn't going to work but thinking, let's see what foolish thing they come up with.

Marilyn told me, "If this is going to work, you need to take the cuff end of the coat sleeve and put it over your face." I didn't like that much since this had been one of Daddy's old chore coats and it smelled like pig slop, sour milk, cow manure and possibly four or five other bad things.

Seeing that I wasn't happy with this new requirement, Marilyn laughed and asked, "Can you see the stars now?" Before I could answer, a very full glass of cold water came pouring down on my face. I really didn't think their little trick was too funny but everyone else got a big laugh from it, even my mother.

I knew someday, I would get even.

Chapter 10

Best Fishing Hole

Another great day in the Flint Hills. I knew today had the makings of a wonderful day. It was the first of May, 1948. When I walked outside, a spring breeze blew in my face with a wonderful feeling of warm air. I looked up to see there were a few fluffy white clouds drifting across the sky.

My dogs ran up to me and began jumping all around with the exception of Old Shep. He just stood there and wagged his tail. He was just too old to jump and carry on like Tubsey and Happy.

My sisters, Frances and Marilyn, had promised we would do something fun today. Maybe we'd go see Mary Bigler or take an exploring trip up into the pasture; I just wasn't sure. I thought we might even go looking for wild strawberries since they were the best tasting berry one could ever experience. The strawberries in Mamma's garden were good, but not as good as those little things growing in the grass near the pond.

Daddy had been in the field already for a couple of hours planting corn when Mamma yelled, "Come in for breakfast." I went in and sat down at my place at the table, and just then my sisters came and sat down also. Mamma gave me a cup of milk in my Roy Rogers cup and poured out some Post Toasties from the box with Roy's picture on it.

I asked Frances and Marilyn what we were going to do today that was a surprise. They explained we were going fishing. This was something new that I had never done before. I started to get excited and many questions came to mind such as: Where? How were we going to get there? What would we use as a fishing pole and the list went on and on.

We finished breakfast and, I must say, I finished in a big hurry. Daddy had gotten the fishing poles down from the barn (which I didn't know we had) and laid them on the hay wagon in the barnyard. They were long bamboo sticks with string, a red and white bobber, sinker, hook and very dusty for having been in the barn, probably for years.

My sisters then told me we had to dig for some worms. I thought this was okay, but wondered where would we do that and what would we put them in. Frances got the shovel and Marilyn found an old tin can that had once contained salmon. We didn't buy much food in tin cans as Mamma put up most of our food in glass jars.

We then went behind the barn in a shady place where the ground was moist and cool. The sisters struggled with the shovel but then finally got it into the ground. Turning the dirt over there was nothing. So, another attempt was made and this time it was easier, and a big fat earthworm appeared. We kept digging for another short period and it was decided we had found enough.

Not only was I going to get to go fishing, I learned how to dig for worms! They were kind of slimy and tried to wiggle out of our hands but I do believe my sisters were much more afraid of them than I was. After all, boys are supposed to be braver than girls around such things like worms, bugs and snakes.

Since we had gotten up fairly early that morning, we still had plenty of time to go fishing before dinner, I was told. So, with fishing poles, worms, and a bucket to bring home any fish we might catch, we were off on our adventure, walking about one-half mile to the creek west of our house.

We crossed the gravel road in front of our place where a gate existed. It was one of those gates made out of barbwire and was held in place with another wire looped over one of the posts that hung on the four-strand barbwire gate. We could not get the wire undone to let the gate down so we relied on the next best thing—we just crawled under it and pulled all of our fishing gear through. To make this easier, my sisters took turns holding the bottom wire up to give more room to crawl under. Now we were in the Christlieb pasture headed for the little creek.

The Flint Hills were lush and green with the grass growing and thousands of colorful wild flowers displaying yellow, white, red and blue blooms. As far as I could see, the green hills met the beautiful light blue sky. A few birds took flight, some low to the ground and others at great heights. There were barn swallows flying just inches above the grass and meadow larks sitting on tall shoots of grass, swaying back and forth. Then I could see and hear crows in the trees down by the creek. We were walking through grass that was up to my waist in some places. I just assumed to get to the good fishing places, you had to make a real effort. It didn't matter because this was my first time and it was exciting.

All of a sudden, I looked down and there was a box turtle trying to make its way through the tall grass. So, I picked it up and it peed on my hand. Dang! I put it in the bucket we had for the fish, if we caught any; I was just trying to be helpful. We trudged on, seeing more beautiful and exciting things every step we took. Then finally we were at the creek. The grass there was fine and soft, and the water was so clear I could see fish and tadpoles. This water was as clear as any I would ever see in any mountain stream, but it just wasn't flowing nearly as fast or as cold.

This was the ideal place to be with lots of trees and leaves just starting to bud. I could see robins making their nest in the branches and watched while they flew away and then returned with a piece of grass or twig for the new nest.

The side of the creek we were on was about the same elevation as the water, but on the other side a limestone outcrop went upward about fifteen feet or so. There were also trees on the opposite side. Right in front of us was a larger pool about thirty feet across and three times that long. At each end there was a small rapid, one letting water in and the other letting water out.

With the warm breeze, the sounds of running water, the smell of green grass growing, the touch of the soft grass near the creek and the eye-catching combination of everything, it was almost perfection. Somehow I realized this would be a good place to come and just sit and take in nature, but a little boy never just sits. Years later, when wanting to just relax and let my mind go to a very peaceful place, this is what I think of and envision.

Even with the beautiful surroundings we were, after all, there to fish. I think I became so excited that I jumped up and down a couple of times. My sisters told me I needed to be quiet and not scare the fish. Next we unrolled the fishing poles and string. It looked like we had a lot of string but since I had never fished before, I had no idea how much was needed.

Now it was time to put the worm on the hook and then set the bobber about two feet from the hook and sinker. The worm thing was a little more difficult than expected. Since the worm was pretty big, long and fat, it had to be pulled apart with just enough to put on the small hook. I let Frances do this for me. She squirmed saying, "Yuck," and did it reluctantly, but what a nice sister!

Finally, we were ready to put the hook, worm, sinker and bobber in the water. Again, with the help of Frances, a success-ful launch was made. The bobber floated very peacefully in the water, and I asked, "Now what do I do?" Both sisters said to "just wait." After probably five minutes, which felt like an hour, the bobber went under and came back up. I had my first fish bite ever! This was exciting and my heart began to race. I was told if the fish pulls the bobber under again, just give it a jerk.

Within a few minutes the bobber went under and I jerked. I mean I really jerked and the bobber, hook, sinker, and worm ended up right at my feet. Then I was told, "You really didn't need to pull quite so hard."

I put the line back into the water and soon it was bobbing up and down again. Eventually I caught a fish. I didn't think I had ever done anything as much fun as this. I caught seven fish that day and all were perch. I guess they were pretty small but they looked big to me.

During the time we were fishing I don't think my sisters put their fishing poles in the water once. They were busy either helping me take fish off the hook or adding a new worm, but they seemed to be having almost as much fun as I was.

When Frances announced it was time for us to go home, I reluctantly agreed. But they had one more thing they wanted to teach me, and it was how to skip a rock across the water. At first I said, "it won't work" because everybody knew if you put a rock in a bucket of water it would sink. I thought it was just another sister-trick and I had better watch out.

Frances found a rock that was pretty flat, and holding it with her finger on the narrow side and twisting her body and arm just right, she threw it towards the water. I'll be; it worked! It must have skipped three or four times. I was anticipating getting wet or some other uncomfortable outcome by being tricked so this was a nice surprise.

I then tried to do what Frances did, but my rocks just went plop into the water and sank, no skipping. Marilyn helped me find a couple of perfect rocks and finally they skipped one time. Victory at last.

Soon we headed back to the house. I turned my box turtle, that I had named Daisy, loose so we could use the bucket to carry the fish. I just couldn't wait to show Mamma what I had caught. Maybe we could have them for supper.

When we got home, Mamma came out to meet us asking, "How did the fishing go?" The dogs came running to see what we had brought home too. After showing her what I caught, I told Mamma hopefully, "We can have them for supper." I was disappointed when she explained that they were too small and would be all bones. In addition, she said she had already planned to have chicken and noodles along with new potatoes and peas. That time of year we also had lettuce, radishes and onions from the garden.

We ate dinner and Mamma asked if I would like to lie down for a nap. I immediately said no, but compromised on lying down for just a few minutes. Instead, I immediately went to sleep and she "forgot" to wake me up when a few minutes went by. I think it was a trick.

Mamma explained to me about polio and why I shouldn't get too tired. I tried to tell her I never got tired and don't worry about me, but I think it went in one of her ears and out the other. That is what she would say when she would tell me what not to do and I went ahead and did it anyway.

After getting up from my nap, with the help of Marilyn, we took the fish out of the bucket and put them into a couple of fruit jars so I could show them to Daddy when he came in from the field. Soon we heard the tractor coming and I went running to where I knew Daddy would park it to take off the corn planter, if he was done. If not done, the tractor would just set there overnight. Daddy pulled up, turned off the engine and then put an old tin can over the exhaust.

I excitedly greeted him to explain about our fishing trip and showed him one of the jars full of fish. He said, "Looks like we will have supper tonight." I didn't want to tell him that Mamma already said no.

Every day after that I begged my sisters to take me fishing, but they never had time. Then one of the neighbor boys, Eddie Aeschliman, came over to our house to spend the day. I thought it would be more fun than anything to take him fishing, but could still not get either of my sisters to go along. A big decision had to be made. Should I go by myself with Eddie or should I not? Well, I made the wrong decision and we went fishing by ourselves.

Soon, nobody could find us and panic set in—the hunt was on. We started home, and to my surprise, my mother and Marilyn met us. My mother was not understanding at all. I got a whipping and was told we could have drowned. Besides being in trouble, we never caught any fish, and the rocks we tried to skip just sank. This wasn't a good day in the Flint Hills. I never went fishing again by myself, I believe, until I was twenty-one years of age.

Chapter 11 ℞

Scariest Time of My Life

Thinking back over my childhood there were a number of moments I remember very distinctly, but one jumped out at me as the scariest of all. I think that if my mother hadn't been there, I would have had a heart attack, or at least wet my pants. That is really scary.

I particularly feared coyotes and their yelping. The first thing that I recall was an evening, probably in the early winter of 1947, and I would have been 3 years old. It was dark outside, there were a few inches of snow on the ground, and the temperature was well below freezing. The moon was full, and along with a sky full of stars, it almost looked like daylight. Mamma, Daddy and I stepped onto the back porch after doing chores, and the screen door closed behind us with a bang. I jumped and bumped into Daddy who was carrying the milk. Because night had fallen, Mamma volunteered, "I'll go find the lamp" and she went inside to search. Rural electricity had not been installed at our place yet and would not arrive for another 18 months.

Standing out on the back porch, I was just a little scared, even though Daddy was right there. Finally, Mamma yelled, "I found the lamp. You can come in now." Just as we stepped in and closed the door, there was the loudest, most blood-curdling, fearsome, coyote scream I have ever heard in my life. I thought it must have been on the back porch with us, or at least it sounded like it was. Later I realized it wasn't.

I let out my own scream and ran to Mamma. She put her arms around me and, sitting down, pulled me upon her lap and gave me a very special hug. In words that were so soothing, she made the fear disappear. I remember saying, "Mamma, that really scared me, and I need your hugs. I love you."

Later, getting everything put away after supper, Daddy commented, "Son, on a night like this when the moon and stars are so bright along with the white snow, it seems like the coyotes are the loudest." Then he added more wood to the stove, and it began to roar and put off a lot of heat. That was good because the house had gotten cold while we were out milking the cows.

Soon, Mamma said it was time for bed and she would read a story to me. When it came time for the story, I asked if she could read the one about Roy Rogers and Dale Evans, which she did. As the night went on, I could still hear the coyotes, but none of them sounded as close as the one when we had just come into the house. There were a few more yelps and I finally drifted off to sleep listening to the wind in the old pear tree just south of the house. It moaned and squeaked as the wind blew and twisted it around.

If you have never heard a coyote or group of coyotes before, just drive out into the countryside near Virgil some winter night, turn off your engine, and listen. It won't be long before you will be starting the engine again. I guarantee you will be scared.

These animals were known by the Aztecs as "tricksters" and "God's dogs." Many attempts have been made to exterminate coyotes and they always flourish. It is known that as the coyote population begins to diminish, they will start having larger litters which will cause their numbers to grow again.

It is my belief that one coyote can make the sound of thirty or so. Whether this is true or not, it seemed believable to a young boy who was standing outside on a cold and dark night when a coyote began its yipping and howling.

We had neighbors who used to go coyote hunting and, at the end of the hunt, hang their kill on a fence post next to the road with the coyote's head hanging down and ears removed. Sometimes there would even be ten to fifteen. The ears were turned into the county for a two-dollar bounty. As a little boy, I never felt sorry for the coyotes, but now I realize they had families too. But why did they have to scare me so much?

The other wildlife that I was afraid of were possums. They were so ugly and played dead if you approached them. If you made them mad, they showed their teeth and hissed. No thanks; I just wanted to stay away from them. I really didn't see them very often, but once was enough.

Chapter 12

Easter Egg Hunt
(The longest Easter egg hunt in history)

Hunting Easter Eggs was an annual ritual that I looked forward to each year, and I could hardly wait for the time to come. My sisters Frances and Marilyn hid the eggs and I would then spend the rest of the day looking for them. Sometimes they wouldn't do a very good job hiding them and I found them fast, thus causing me to beg my sisters to hide them again. In other words, I became a pain.

I had to resort to some drastic methods to get my way like tying my sisters to their chairs while they were studying or sometimes just begging Mamma to make them do what I wanted. A younger brother had to be very creative and resourceful. Living on a farm and being the only child was different than living with a number of children around the same age. If I didn't entertain myself, I became bored.

Of course, prior to the hunt, the first thing that needed to be done was to gather the eggs from the chicken house. Mamma did this because I was afraid to. I wasn't going to stick my hand under those old hens. They might peck me, or maybe worse, there could be a snake under them. I never heard of it happening, but I was able to create all kinds of images in my mind, so I just let Mamma do it. When we gathered eggs for coloring, we got a lot. After all, they were free, at least for me. It was not unusual to start with two or three dozen at a time.

A day or two before coloring, Mamma would go to the Commons' Store in Virgil and buy the coloring tablets. There were usually five or six colors. You put a colored tablet in a cup and poured boiling water over it, filling the cup. The tablet would then dissolve and create a colored liquid.

There was also a wax pencil that was included. With this pencil you could make all kinds of designs. If you knew how to write your name you could put that on the eggs too. Unfortu-nately, for a few years I didn't know how to write my name, so Mamma would do this for me. You had to put the eggs in the cup of hot water for a minute or two before taking them out to let them dry, but it only took a little while.

Mamma always helped me find a basket to put all the eggs in so they would be easy to carry. They were now ready for my sisters to hide the eggs around the house and wash shed, but never in the garden. The best places for hiding the eggs were in the lilac bushes, around the propane tank, by the cellar door, next to the old cistern, by the water pump, by the fence posts going around the front yard, in the iris beds, and under the front porch. But my sisters also found many more places.

I think it was my last year to hunt eggs that the longest Eas-ter Egg hunt came about. It was a couple of weeks after Easter and the eggs were becoming pretty dirty and a number of them had cracked. They even began to smell bad. I really had to beg for hours to get my sister Marilyn to hide the eggs just one more time. She did it reluctantly. I think she was determined to hide them so well I would be looking for weeks to find them all. It was getting late in the evening and when she was done, I only had about a half hour to hunt. Of course, she knew I was scared of the dark and wouldn't be looking too long. So, I found a few and went inside the house.

The following morning, I resumed the hunt. Much to my sur-prise I found only a few more eggs, but I continued to look day after day and really never gave up, even looking weeks later.

Since I didn't understand why I couldn't find more eggs, I finally came to a couple of conclusions months later. Since we had coyotes, possums, skunks, and our farm dogs, I thought maybe they had found and eaten them. Then years later anoth-er possibility occurred to me. Maybe Marilyn had fed most of them to the hogs. As aforementioned, hogs will eat anything. A sister who was extremely tired of hiding eggs that should have been thrown away a week earlier, might think of doing just that.

Chapter 13

Rp

Ultimate Payback

It was the heart of summer and the family had gathered to-gether to put up the hay crop. Marilyn and Frances both still lived at home, but Lola and Freda had come to help. Hay harvesting time was like a family gathering with work involved, but so much fun. This was what life and family on the farm was all about.

It was a hot, sunny day with few clouds overhead but there was a slight breeze. It was a day of low humidity so the hay that was cut the day prior, was dry enough to start baling almost as soon as the sun came up. My dad had previously made sure the tractors were gassed up and the baler was properly greased along with the other equipment. He also had done all the morning chores except milking the cows, and Mamma had done that while 13-year-old Marilyn made breakfast. Daddy had gone to the hayfield with the rake to turn the hay, but was back in time to eat before any of the help started to arrive around 8 a.m.

Frances worked in the hayfield with the men. She drove the tractor, pulling the John Deere baler. This was what happened to a girl born into a family with no older boys. My father was extremely proud of his family and, as aforementioned, daughter Frances. He was known to say she could drive the tractor to the baler better than any man he knew. When Daddy bought her the tractor umbrella to provide protection from the blistering sun, it made Frances feel special. Our father was very proud of all his children and complemented us every time he got a chance, and it was not unusual for him to brag about us also.

About 7:45 am, the help started rolling in. First to arrive were my sister Freda and her husband Floyd Wayne; and Dale Sauder, boyfriend of my sister Marilyn.

The baler needed two men, one on each side—one to push the wire through and one to tie the wire off, plus move a wooden bale divider. What a dirty job that was! All of the dirt coming off the ground and hay created a constant dirt storm. The guys working this position would come out at the end of the day as black as I think possible.

The rest of the crew loaded the baled hay onto wagons for transporting to the barn and stacking. This made a pretty good-sized crew, and they all had to be fed at dinner time along with cold drinks during the day. This kept my other sisters busy working with Mamma or just visiting, which was one of the pleasures of getting together.

This left me totally bored. Leaving alone a young four-year-old boy with nothing to do and everyone occupied, sets up a difficult situation. Something has to give. I first thought my best place was down at the hayfield which was the opposite of what my parents, and probably my sisters, would think.

With no one to supervise me, it was time to take things into my own hands. I knew I couldn't actually go to the hayfield because I would get in trouble, so I decided to just disappear and, sooner or later, they would come looking for me. This was a plan that took patience, which has been a weak point all my life.

I first had to find a hiding spot where I could watch all the activity as they hunted for me. The perfect spot happened to be in a fairly good-sized Lilac bush about twenty-five feet from the backdoor of the house. Getting into a good sitting position was important because the backdoor was the only one anyone ever came in or out of. Now it was the time to just wait and it didn't take long before the search was on.

My mother told Marilyn to go find me. She came outside and yelled, "Robert. Robert, where are you?" Of course, there was no response from me because the fun had just started. Marilyn went back inside and I guess told my mother I couldn't be found. She hadn't looked very hard. After a minute or two, Mamma came outside and yelled, "Robert, Robert, where are you?" Not responding gave me satisfaction that my plan was working. I'll teach them to just ignore me during such exciting happenings like the hay harvest!

Soon, there were Mamma and my sisters, all outside looking for me. They went to the milk house, barn, chicken house, privy, washhouse, and even the root cellar. My mother finally said, "Let's look down in the cistern" which had a very heavy top on it that took two of them to lift off.

Of course, I wasn't there either. I always wondered how they thought I could get that lid off, fall in and then put the lid back in place. But you never know what a group of women will come up with when left by themselves to fret and worry. Marilyn said, "Well, at least you know he will come in when it gets dark because he is a real scaredy cat of the dark." Mamma replied to Marilyn that this was no time to be making fun of Robert, and to "remember that little Aeschliman boy who got killed last year."

After much searching, Mamma finally gave a sigh and said, "Okay, we better go down and see if Robert made his way to the hayfield." She asked Marilyn to walk down there and check with Daddy. Reluctantly and grumbling, my sister headed toward the hayfield. It was a pretty long walk and took somewhere close to an hour to get there and back. My only thought was that my plan was really working...they won't ignore me again. What a trick on them!

About an hour later, Marilyn came back and reported, "Daddy hasn't seen him at all." They went inside except for Freda who remained outside walking around. I had reached a point that I could no longer sit perfectly still and so I moved just a little and made a small noise, like a snake going through the leaves. But Freda heard it and screamed. I just couldn't hold it in and laughed. I was found. Now angered, Freda yelled, "He's out here."

My mother and other sisters came running outside as Freda began looking for a switch. "I am going to whip him so bad he doesn't do this again."

Thank goodness for motherly love. My Mamma stepped in to intervene and said she was very worried, but so happy I was found. "No, he won't be whipped." Instead, Mamma told Marilyn she needed to go down and tell Daddy that "Robert has been found." She was lucky to catch a hay wagon returning to the field, and then caught another coming back to the barn so she didn't have to walk the long distance. For years, Freda told everyone she wanted to give me a whipping that I would remember, but her mother wouldn't let her.

The point to this story is that a bored boy with too much time on his hands, spells T-R-O-U-B-L-E!

I can truthfully say I never did this trick again but oh, how it had worked! This story was probably retold throughout the years many times; It ranked up there with the fire-building story told by my sister on the morning of my birth.

Chapter 14

Saturday Night in Virgil

Saturday night on Main Street in Virgil was a social ritual that had been going on for years during the summer months, but was somewhat limited during the winter. This type of informal gathering also took place in hundreds of other small towns around America the Beautiful. Conversations were usually locally-oriented, and many times family-related. It just felt good having someone other than your immediate family to talk with; there was a lot in common with the other people in the area.

A lot of interdependence took place in our small community because, if your crops didn't have any rain, neither did your neighbors; and thus, if the farmers didn't have any crops to sell merchants, it would definitely be felt. In addition, if a tragedy happened in the community, everyone felt it. As was the case of Lynn Clark, Jimmy Aeschliman, Floyd Hawkins, and Pat Hosack who lost their lives during the period I lived in Virgil.

There was one Saturday night in the summer evening of 1949 when I was 4 years old, which I remember distinctly. Mamma reminded me, "Robert, don't forget this afternoon we are going into town for shopping. You will need to take a bath." After all, it was Saturday and we always took baths on that day, a ritual that never changed. I wasn't sure the bath was needed, but Saturday was bath-day anyway.

The big boiler was filled with water, carried from the well outside, and put on the kitchen stove. The fire was lit and about an hour later, the water became hot enough to put in the tub.

As usual, a tub was brought in from the wash house and set in the middle of the kitchen. This was one of the tubs that Mamma used for the weekly clothes washing. It was round and galvanized with sides about eighteen inches high. It was no wonder we took baths only once a week because of all the work that went in to getting everything ready.

Robert standing on bumper, family car, 1939 Plymouth.

My sisters were the first to take their baths, followed by Mamma and then me. Daddy was the last. Something was said about me being dirtier than my sisters so that was why I fell into the order of bathing next to last. The previous year, the order of baths went a little differently. I took my bath first and my sisters would say, "Robert, don't you pee in the bath water." Now why would I do that?

Finally, it was my turn. Mamma added more hot water and I got in and started washing with a washrag and bar of soap. I washed all the parts I thought were important when Mamma yelled to Marilyn, who was cleaning the cream separator, "You make sure he washes his ears." Marilyn immediately turned toward me and said in a threatening tone, "You heard what Mamma said."

"Yes, I heard her, I always do a good job," but it's hard to see those ears!

Finally, I stood up in the washtub to dry off and stepped over the tub rim to get out. Marilyn said again in a raised voice, "Robert, you're getting water everywhere! You are supposed to dry your feet first." Now how could a person do that when they were still in the water? Sisters just don't understand.

After all the baths, the water was becoming a different color—it was gray with a film that made a ring around the tub. There was only one bath to go and that was Daddy.

Daddy came in and took his bath, Mamma added some more hot water and Daddy asked Mamma to wash his back. He looked like a big white bear. His body was very white, but his hands, arms, neck and face were brown. The top of his head was also white, and his back was very hairy. What a sight! My daddy, the bear.

That afternoon, Mamma fixed Navy beans with pork and corn bread, along with sliced tomatoes and sweet corn on the cob. This was an exceptionally good supper. Of course, I had to add ketchup to my beans. I added ketchup to almost all of my meals except for mashed potatoes and gravy, but I did try it once.

At last, everyone loaded into the four-door, 1939 Plymouth with running boards—me in the front seat with my parents, and sisters in the back seat. The number of sisters who went with us was determined by whether they had dates with boys or something planned with other friends. Frances also sometimes worked at the Pennebaker Store. We usually left late afternoon but not dark yet, down the county roads with dust flying from behind and gravel hitting the undercarriage of the car.

We hadn't gone more than a half mile when my mother looked down at me sitting between her and Daddy and said, "Oh my gosh, Robert, that is the dirtiest ear I think I have ever seen." Out came her handkerchief, she spit on it, and the scrubbing started. How that hurt! Then she turned my head so she could see the other ear and expressed her displeasure saying," This one is even dirtier." Marilyn chimed in, "I told him to wash his ears. He just doesn't listen."

I was happy to get to the old black bridge because I knew we were getting close to town, and I wanted to get out of that car before Mamma found some other place that was dirty on me. Scrubbing hurt! We drove across the railroad tracks and now we were about to town.

Daddy drove up close to the Commons' Store and found a good parking spot. People had started to come and go, and as we pulled in, I heard someone say, "How is the Phillips family today?" Daddy replied, "We are good; how about your family?" Seeing and greeting people went on most of the evening.

The men leaned or sat on cars and visited. It was not unusual to see two or three men around one car, standing, leaning or maybe sitting. It seemed that the running board was a good place to rest your foot.

Most of these men were either smoking or chewing tobacco. I believe that more men chewed than smoked. They almost all wore bib overalls. This was what we would call a Norman Rockwell moment, so homey and down to earth. There were many scenes like this scattered all around Virgil every Saturday night.

Women inside the stores shopped until all was done, and then they formed their groups to visit. Seldom did a woman join the men before it was time to go home. When finished with their visits, the wives found their husbands and announced, "It's getting late and morning will come early. We need to get headed home."

It was a gathering of almost the whole community after a hard week of work. The people were tired but wanted to get out and socialize, plus get those much-needed supplies. In retrospect, I think the number of supplies purchased was probably very minimal. In my family's case, the shopping included maybe a ten-pound bag of sugar and a larger bag of flour, or possibly a new spool of thread and a zipper for a dress my mother was making for one of my sisters.

These Saturday night socials happened countless times throughout the Midwest, from the turn of the century through the late 1950's. Saturday night in Virgil was probably not much different from the Saturday night in numerous small farm towns across the Midwest. Street lights were very few, but the light streaming out of the stores provided plenty of opportunity to see clearly. There was also a special sound emitted with everyone visiting, the few cars moving up and down the street, and the kids running barefoot and laughing. Now and then, you might even hear a dog barking or a cat fight.

It just felt good to be with friends, families and neighbors. You might see people sometimes only once or twice during summer and others every Saturday night. You soon learned where different families hung out along the main street. There was no TV or the many things we have to keep us as busy as we are today. It was a slower time and, in many ways, a better life than today.

A few years earlier, during World War II, there was gasoline rationing and you might even see a team of horses with a wagon tied up to one of the awning posts that hung over the front of the store. I was told by Lucille Aeschliman that during the war, to conserve gasoline, her father Harvey hitched up the horses to the old steel-wheel hayrack and the whole family would head to town. Harvey stood up at the front of the wagon and everyone else's legs hung over the side for the approximate two-mile trip. That way, they had more gasoline to put in the tractor for farming.

Virgil only had a two-block business trade area on Main Street with a grocery store in each block, the Commons' Store on the south end and the Pennebaker Store on the north. My sister Frances worked for Frank Pennebaker as a checkout clerk. She always said what a nice person he was and great to work for. She was working to pay for college tuition. The next year she would graduate from high school and start attending Emporia State Teachers College, working toward a degree in education. My mother often found her way into the Pennebaker Store for something before the night was over, if for no other reason than to say hello to Frances.

I usually got a bottle of strawberry pop, or maybe a small cup of ice cream to be eaten with a little wooden spoon. They each cost a nickel and the ice cream had a picture of a cowboy on the inside of the lid. If you were lucky, you might get Hopalong Cassidy.

Once in a while, my mother would tell me to go find my father and tell him she needed a dollar. So off I'd go looking for him. This probably meant running into the next block to find him standing and leaning against a car, or maybe sitting on the ledge of some storefront talking with a neighbor. "Daddy, Mamma wants a dollar," I'd say and then it was off to make my delivery. This happened quite a few times during the summer and I suddenly had an idea. Why not go to my father, tell him Mamma wanted a dollar, keep the money, and I would be rich? Just the perfect crime. Everything went as planned except I never felt rich; I just ended up feeling guilty.

Virgil had two places to see movies on Saturday night but I don't think they were both open at the same time. One was in a building close to the Pennebaker Store, and the other was in the street in a tent, just south of the Commons' Store. I only attended one movie in the building and none in the tent. I'm not sure if it was the lack of money or my parents did not want to stay in town until it was over. Daddy was always thinking about the chores, even those coming up the next day. He knew he would be up and outdoors to do them by 4 am.

The one in the tent really was not a total tent but only a canvas wall that went around the seating area. There was a truck which held the projector and, at the other end, a big screen and the top was wide open. Folding chairs were setup inside the enclosed area. I was told by some of the older boys they got into the movie free for helping to set up and take down the tent and chairs. This was a good deal because it cost ten cents to get in.

One of the interesting stories told by my sister Frances was that her friend Pearl Wolcott, whose father was the EUB (Evangelical United Brethren) Church Pastor, would not allow her to go to the movies even though the tent was setup in the street in front of their house and church. So, Pearl being creative, would go to the church, crawl up the ladder in the bell tower, and find a place she could sit and watch the movie. This seemed like a good alternative idea to me. Her father would be preparing for the next day's sermon so she would not be missed. I'm sure she didn't think this was a sin. I didn't anyway. But what does a little boy know who can't even get his ears clean?

On the way home, my mother and father always discussed who they had seen plus what was talked about. I guess it was like getting community news from two different sources. Soon we were on the road home and then about to the old black bridge when my father asked, "Mabel, what did you need the dollar for that Robert got from me?"

I was caught with no place to hide or run, so silence came over me. I really don't remember what I said or what my parents said to me. But the lesson learned that night was: Parents talk to each other and you should never try to fool them because you will always end up on the losing end. In addition, you will feel really bad about yourself.

We got home and after the groceries were put away, Mamma put me in bed and gave me a loving kiss. Lying there for a long time, I was feeling really bad that I had done such a stupid thing. Hearing the coyotes yip and carry on, I finally drifted off to sleep.

The wonderful small-town tradition of the Saturday night gathering on Main street was headed for extinction. The television had been invented in the 1920s but did not reach small-town America until the early 1950s. I believe that television was one of the biggest reasons that the Saturday night gatherings started to dwindle, along with the movement of a large number of people from rural areas to the much more populated centers. In the case of Virgil, it was Wichita and Kansas City. In addition, people in these places started working forty-hour weeks and had more money for entertainment. They wanted to spend their time on the weekend doing other things besides shopping.

Thus, stores started staying open later on Thursday evenings throughout the United States. In my opinion, this was one of the causes signaling our society was starting to decline.

Chapter 15

The Cowboy

The lyrics composed by Gene Autry alongside Ray Whitney in the 1939 classic song, "Back in the Saddle Again," spoke to me. In fact, it described me perfectly or, at least, the cowboy I wanted to be.

I think my desire and passion to become a cowboy was a little unusual, but it started early. I was born in the right place in the Flint Hills and that might have been a good start, but we lived on a farm and not a ranch. My father never wore cowboy boots or a cowboy hat, and our horses were of the draft-type for farming.

I think my first exposure to cowboys was in a book one of my aunts gave to me at the age of three titled, *What Do You Want to Be When You Grow Up?* I believe the choices were a doctor, fireman, policeman or a cowboy. From just looking at the pictures, I immediately knew I wanted to be a cowboy. The cowboy had a horse and was roping a young calf. In addition, it wasn't long before I started seeing Roy Rogers on the Post Toasties cereal boxes. And then, more small books about Roy Rogers and Dale Evans made their way to my book collection. At the same time, I fell in love with horses. So, it was just a natural thing...I was going to be a cowboy.

I did see one movie early on in the Virgil movie theater. The movie made a major impression on me and it was a Western. I loved all the horses, cowboy hats, cowboys riding fast chasing cattle, and pretty girls. What could be more exciting? Besides, being outside was wonderful.

One day before I started school in 1950, Sonny Sage and a friend of his rode across the valley to see my sisters. As they rode up on their good-looking horses, outfitted with handsome bridles and saddles seated on a colorful saddle blanket, I was taken aback. They wore long sleeved shirts and Wrangler blue jeans, and great-looking white cowboy hats. They had their hair cut short and looked the epitome of my idols. That was what I wanted…to be a cowboy like them.

From then on, I told Mamma to only buy me Wrangler jeans. I got a black, cowboy straw hat and a red bandana to complete my look. I also had a rope, I think, as soon as I could carry it. It was one my father had around the farm. I roped everything, including my sisters and dogs, but I could never catch a cat. Eventually, when I came outside with my rope, the dogs took off. They just weren't into this roping thing at all.

Then came the designing of my branding iron when I was about five years old. It was a takeoff of my father's WP (his initials) and Roy Rogers RR bar, mine being RP. This brand was never registered, but a branding iron was made much later in my life which I still have today and hangs here in my office.

In my early life as a cowboy, I only had a stick horse which was not satisfactory; it was slow but, at least, never threw me off. I really wanted a horse and probably asked my mother and father for one at least once a day. I wanted it to be a palomino, just like Roy's horse Trigger.

I never listened to our radio very much but loved to hear Gene Autry sing, "Back in the Saddle Again" as cited at the beginning of this chapter. And then he came out with "Rudolph the Red Nosed Reindeer." It wasn't a cowboy song, but it was Gene Autry and I loved Christmas, especially Santa Claus.

When Christmas came, I got my first Gene Autry cap gun and holster. What a gift! I immediately started working on my quick draw but soon decided that I better be nice to everyone and offer to buy a round of milk every time I got a chance, or maybe strawberry pop.

Virgil was a good place for a cowboy to grow up. If you were lucky, you might see the Kimbells driving their cattle to the railroad for shipment to Kansas City. It seemed like everyone had at least a few beef cattle around their place, the same as we did. Virgil had a stockyard at the train depot just like Abilene, Elsworth and Dodge City.

I learned later that they shipped hogs out of these stockyards also, but who wants to be a hog boy? Besides, those hogs really smelled terrible. In my very earliest days, I believed that a big hog might even eat a little boy. If you ever watch a bunch of hogs eat, you would know why I had that fear. They will almost kill each other getting to what was given them out of the slop bucket which was full of lots of gross, smelly things.

After I finally got a horse, she was afraid of hogs too. Regardless, I dreamed of riding my horse on the trail with a few of my cowboy friends and stopping overnight by some beautiful stream with a few trees for shade. Then, after unsaddling and brushing our horses down, we would sit around the campfire roasting hot dogs. What a fun thing that would be to do! The only problem at that time was that I didn't have any friends who had horses. And for a couple of years, I didn't have one either.

It's strange now to think how much of a disaster it would have been, lying out there under the stars, if a coyote came into camp and started yipping. Oh well, I think the campfire would have kept them scared off.

Chapter 16

A Visit to Meet Grandma

It was four in the morning during the summer of 1947. The morning air was still and the humidity was high. A small amount of light was peeking from the darkness, causing a red glow in the eastern sky and the stars were starting to fade. Far off in the distance I could hear a lone coyote crying out for its mate.

My family and I were preparing to leave on a trip to the Norton State Tuberculosis Sanatorium in Norton, Kansas about 325 miles away. Mamma had loaded the car the night before with a number of things she thought we might need, but the majority of things were to be loaded that morning. Suit cases, jugs of water, blankets, a couple boxes of food were all loaded just before leaving.

This was a trip my mother had been planning for months, if not years. She hadn't seen her mother for more than five years and she was anxious to see her, especially to introduce her little boy to her mother. And, of course, let me meet Grandma Young for the first time.

The planning it took for us to be gone a whole week in the summer time was quite a task. The corn had to be laid aside. The hay had to be baled, and then someone had to be found who could come milk the cows twice a day, collect the eggs, and feed the chickens and the hogs in addition to the dogs and cats.

This planning had to be very flexible depending on the weather. There was always a concern as to what would happen if it rained and the hay couldn't be put up, or maybe it was too wet to cultivate the corn. Lastly, what if someone got sick?

My grandmother Young was in a tuberculous hospital, and had been for a number of years. I had never seen her before and I was three years old. I knew she was special since my mother wrote her often and was always extremely excited when she received a letter in return.

The car was packed with enough clothes, food and other necessities to be gone about a week. On this particular trip were my mother, father, sister Freda and her two-year-old daughter Judy, my sisters Frances and Marilyn, and me. The car was full with Daddy, Mamma and me in the front seat and the others in the back. The inside was very spacious. It also had wing-windows that could be adjusted to direct a lot of air inside. This feature came in very handy on hot days, and we experienced a lot of those on this trip.

We pulled out of the barnyard onto the gravel road just as the sunrays started shooting across the morning sky. What a beautiful time of the morning! Everyone was excited, especially Mamma. I think this was one of the happiest times I ever saw her.

The first town we came to was Hamilton which we reached by traveling over a gravel road in need of grading. The recent rain in the past week created the plentiful and deep ruts that caused us to bounce around quite a lot. We finally came to a stop sign, giving Daddy the opportunity to open his door and spit his mouthful of tobacco out. Mamma just frowned, showing her displeasure.

Once we got through Hamilton, Daddy told us that the rest of the way should be paved. He was right; it was paved but most of the highway needed a great deal of repair. World War II had only been over a couple of years and nothing had been done since the start of the war. Potholes in the asphalt and deteriorating shoulders, or no shoulders at all, made for very slow going. Most of the ditches on each side of the highway needed mowing and almost everything needed attention.

When we had been on the road for 56 miles, just a little longer than two and one-half hours, we came to El Dorado. Entering the town, Daddy saw a small diner and parked so we could go in. Eating any place other than home was unusual for our family because we hardly ever ate out, as it just cost too much. This was possibly my first time ever eating at any kind of commercial establishment. We went inside and there was not a table big enough to hold all seven of us so we each took a stool at the counter. I sat between Mamma and Daddy.

To get an early start, Daddy had gotten up about two in the

morning to milk the cows and, since we left early, it was already decided to stop for breakfast along the road. Daddy always wanted to get started as soon as he could saying, "The sooner we get there the sooner we can start home." This was a motto he always lived by: the first to arrive, never late, but the first to leave. Even though we were going to be gone for a week, Daddy still wanted to get that early start.

When it became my turn to order food, I chose a hamburger. Mamma was surprised and asked if I was sure I didn't want eggs or pancakes. I told her adamantly, "No, I want a hamburger." I thought hamburgers were about the greatest thing you could eat. In fact, one of my goals as a young child was to be able to have enough money to eat hamburgers any time I wanted. Not a real big aspiration like finding a cure for cancer, but I was just three years old, after all, and eating was pretty important to me.

The waitress explained they did not serve hamburgers that early in the day but she would ask if an exception could be made. I insisted and finally got my hamburger. When the waitress asked, "Would you like anything on your hamburger?" I quickly replied, "ketchup." I was a purest when it came to condiments, and ketchup was the only thing that could make a burger better. At home I even ate bread with only ketchup as a sandwich and thought it was really good so this was the best breakfast I could imagine—a hamburger with ketchup. I thought this was a wonderful start to this trip.

After breakfast we resumed our trip to Norton, but we planned to stop about halfway and stay with one of Daddy's aunts and her husband who lived on a wheat farm just six miles east of Larned. As we proceeded on, and as the day warmed up, it started to get hot in the car. The air also began to feel much dryer and there was not a cloud in the sky. Fortunately, Mamma had prepared a number of water jars for us to drink as we went along. Daddy also suggested that those car wing-windows be opened to put a breeze across the inside. We opened them but the breeze was still really quite warm, almost like standing by the potbelly stove.

At dinnertime we stopped at a small roadside park. It had just one picnic table and a couple of trees. Mamma, with the help of my sisters, spread out the food she had prepared for the trip. We ate and walked around to stretch our legs, knowing we still had a long way to go before reaching Aunt Eva's and Uncle William's place.

We finally loaded up and started down the highway again. It was almost unbearable with no clouds to block the sun and heat. I was about to experience something that I had never seen before.

About a quarter to a half-mile ahead, there appeared a lake of water that went across the highway. I was confused. "Mamma, do you see that water across the road in front of us?" She gave a little laugh and answered, "That is a mirage." Of course, I asked what a mirage was. Mamma tried to explain that a mirage is seeing something you think is there but it really isn't. "It happens out here in Western Kansas a lot. It is caused by heat rising off the ground and the sun shining through it." As we got closer, the water just seemed to disappear. I was still confused and didn't understand, but I wanted to make sure Mamma knew it didn't make sense to me. As we proceeded across the sand hills and it got hotter, we saw a few more mirages. Later in life I learned that this area was considered to be the great desert by some early pioneers and I understood why—hot, dry and not very appealing.

Traveling had been slow, going through all the small towns. Most of the places were a little bigger than Virgil, but not by much. They all seemed very prosperous. Most of the store buildings were full and there were three or four gas stations in each town. Sometimes there was parking in the center of the main street, and at other times parking was only in front of the stores. All the towns were very busy with people coming and going, and kids running along with their parents. Once in a while we would see two or three kids on bicycles. I recall Daddy commenting, "Looks like people around here have a little money. The wheat crop must have been good here this year."

Finally by late afternoon, we neared a driveway going into a wheat field. There we turned and followed it up to a house and barn. Daddy announced, "We are here."

When we all got out of the car and started stretching our legs, Aunt Eva came out to meet us. She was a little woman with gray hair pulled back into a bun. She also had a big smile and greeted us by saying, "Bill, it is sure nice to see you and your wonderful family. This must be Robert that Mabel wrote me about." She wore a fairly plain dress that was neatly pressed and hung almost all the way to the ground, plus a nice-looking apron with lace around it. Later I learned they were very successful wheat farmers, and the price of wheat had been very good since just after the war.

There were few trees to be seen except for a row of very tall cottonwoods on the west side of the drive which had been planted there years ago. Everything else was wheat fields or a small amount of grassland. You could see for a long way as it was really flat. Then, looking up into the trees, I could see crows...just like the ones we had at home.

Aunt Eva invited everyone into the house where she had iced tea and water ready for us. It was cooler in the house, if for no other reason than just being out of the bright sun. It wasn't long before I was outside exploring the barnyard which wasn't too exciting because they had no animals, just fields of wheat.

Aunt Eva set supper on the table. Uncle William said grace and everyone sat down to eat. A lot of lively conversation occurred as we ate, and when supper was over, Aunt Eva brought out a couple of apple pies.

After we finished eating, the men went outside, including Judy and me. The two of us explored more of the barnyard while Daddy and Uncle William stood there talking about farming, particularly wheat farming.

Daddy, before getting married, had come out here to assist his family with the wheat harvest when most everything was done by horsepower. Daddy even told me that he would ride his horse all the way here and it would take him three or four days, just sleeping in people's barnyards as he went along. He said that most people would invite him in for supper and provide him some grain and hay for his horse. I thought that would be a real adventure. Where do I sign up?

At last, it was bedtime. There weren't enough beds for everyone so I slept on the floor in the bedroom with my parents. In the other bedroom, Freda and Frances slept in the bed and Marilyn and Judy slept on the floor. Morning came too early as far as I was concerned, but Daddy was true to his traveling motto and insisted we must get on the road.

After Aunt Eva served us breakfast and the dishes were washed, the car was loaded, and we bid Aunt Eva and Uncle William farewell promising to "see you in a few days." We drove toward the west, heading again now for Norton. We had traveled about 191 miles our first day and had only about 150 miles to go.

The trip on the second day was almost like the first except it was over different highways and shorter. We reached Larned and stopped at a store to buy things for the dinner meal to eat at a roadside park. There, we chose a picnic table with one lone tree providing shade, and not much of that, but I saw the most amazing thing.

I saw an animal that was about the size of a small dog, with ears that hung down to almost touch the ground, and it jumped a long distance each time it moved. I said, "Daddy, look at that strange thing over there." Daddy laughed and said, "Son, that is a jackrabbit; they are all over western Kansas…in the millions." When the rabbits ran, their ears stood up straight and they seemed to lope along like a horse. The jackrabbits were ugly, unlike the cute little cottontail rabbits we had back home. I soon had enough of these strange creatures and was glad we weren't there long and on the road again.

We arrived in Norton about 5 pm—tired, hot and hungry. We stayed in an old hotel downtown that had a big room where you checked in. The building looked old, but not as old as our home back at Virgil. This was my first time to ever stay in a hotel.

We took two rooms: Mamma, Daddy, and me in one; Freda, Judy, Frances and Marilyn in another. I was surprised neither of the rooms had an outhouse. Instead, a toilet was down the hall about forty-feet and even had a shower with it. I was excited by all of this and amused my parents when I said, "This is great; we don't have to go outside, and it doesn't smell like our little house at home." I went on saying, "They even have toilet paper like the gas stations instead of catalogs like we use in the little house."

The hotel seemed to be cooler inside. It had a lot of tall windows and the ceilings were high but there was no air conditioning, only electric fans. We didn't mind because we didn't have air conditioning at home since we still didn't have electricity.

Norton was a nice town about twice the size of Virgil. It sat on US Highway 36 that crosses the northern part of Kansas from east to west. The Tuberculosis Hospital was located approximately five miles east of Norton, and sat on a ten-acre, tree-covered campus consisting of a number of redbrick two-story buildings. We arrived in Norton too late in the day to go see Grandma, so it was decided to go to the hospital the following morning.

For breakfast the next morning we went to a small café down the street. They had a table big enough to accommodate all of us and again I had a hamburger. That, of course, surprised the waitress and she asked me, "Are you sure?" Marilyn piped up and commented, "He is strange but we put up with him," making everyone laugh but me.

After breakfast, we headed for the hospital. Going east on US 36 we could see a number of tall redbrick buildings. Daddy finally announced, "This must be it," and proceeded to pull into the driveway and stop in front of the big building. Mamma suggested, "Bill, why don't you and I go in and see what we have to do to see Mamma?"

I found this kind of strange for my mother to be calling someone Mamma. I wondered, do old people have mammas too? I had never seen my grandmother, even though I was almost four years old. My Grandmother Young had been confined to this hospital about a year prior to my birth. It was also the first time since she was admitted that Mamma was able to visit...a visit longtime in coming.

Soon after entering the big building, my parents came out of the doors and headed for the car. Mamma said, "We are going to park over there and they will bring Mamma out so we can sit there under the trees." She was pointing to a group of chairs in the shade.

I had only seen pictures of my grandmother so I was a little shy in meeting my only living grandparent. She looked frail and weak, walking very slowly and needing help from a hospital staff member, and then help from Mamma and Freda.

I really didn't know what to expect when I saw her. Then

Robert, Mother, and Grandmother taken at the Norton TB Hospital.

there she was—an older woman who was hunched over, looking very frail with a wrinkled face and somewhat sunken eyes surrounded by dark circles. Her cheek bones protruded and her mouth was somewhat sunken, like she didn't have any teeth. She spoke quietly and it was a little difficult for me to hear what she said. Whenever she tried to walk, she needed her cane, with Mamma and Freda on each side. Still, she did have a smile on her face and we could tell she was happy to see us. At one point, she reached out and patted me on the head saying, "Robert sure looks like a fine boy."

Everyone crowded around her, giving hugs and saying how great it was to see her and finally be here. I hung back not knowing exactly what to do or what to say.

Soon everyone moved to the chairs and began taking pictures with a black box-type of thing they called a Kodak camera while the talk just kept going. The laughter was everywhere and everyone was having a wonderful time.

Judy and I, not too much in the conversation, would drift off exploring whatever we could, but we knew to remain within sight of the grownups. We ran and chased each other as kids will do. No one was allowed to go inside the hospital except to use the restrooms and they were located close to the front doors.

Mamma had brought food for us to eat dinner with Grandma so we could have the maximum time with her. But afternoon came and it was time for us to leave for the day. Grandma was getting tired and it was also getting hot so we knew it was time for her to return to the hospital. We then loaded into the car and headed for the hotel. Since there was also still a fear of polio, Mamma insisted that Judy and I rest and hopefully take a nap.

The next day was almost a repeat of the prior, but when they brought Grandma out of the hospital, she was carrying something in her hand. We quickly went to greet her and were happy to see her again. After making our way to the chairs and seating Mamma and Grandma, Grandma called me to her and said, "Robert, I have something for you. Your mother wrote me that you are very scared of the dark, so I have this for you." She then handed me a small flashlight saying, "I hope this will help." My mother reminded me, "Robert, now what do we say?"

She really didn't need to because I knew just what to say. "Oh, Grandma, thank you so much!"

We didn't have flashlights at home; we just had kerosene lanterns and I was too young to light them. Mamma never wanted me to use the matches so this was just the perfect gift!

Later after dinner, a disaster occurred when Judy fell while holding a glass pop bottle, cutting her hand badly. I had been chasing Judy and she fell down trying to get away from me. Having pop was unusual because it cost a nickel a bottle so it was considered a very special treat. Judy's mother Freda and Frances took her to the restroom to thoroughly wash the cut, and then wrapped it in a clean dish rag that Mamma had brought with us. That afternoon, when we returned to Norton, we stopped at the drug store to get some iodine to put on the cut. It was serious enough that today she would have gotten stitches, I am sure. But things were different in those days and we handled wounds as best we could. There would be no more running and chasing each other on this trip. Especially with glass in our hands.

The next day was our last day to visit so we made it back to the hospital. It was almost a repeat of the previous two days, but without anyone falling down and getting hurt. Judy's cut hurt and she wasn't feeling well, and it didn't help that the heat was so oppressive.

When it was time for the goodbyes, there was a lot of sadness. It had been almost five years since anyone had seen Grandma and no one had any idea when the next time would be. But it had been so good to see her and express our love.

It was, of course, not known then, but Mamma would never see her mother alive again. I thought about my grandmother and how she was the person Mamma would have gone to when she was hurt as a little girl, and I remembered that she was also the one who wrote the special poem when I was born.

When we went back to the hotel, Judy and I took another nap which was a good idea since Daddy wanted to get another early start the next morning. While he always wanted an early start, most of all, he hoped to beat what heat we could. Starting off about 5 am we headed back to stay at Uncle William's and Aunt Eva's, but this time we got there earlier.

After spending the night, we got another very early start and made it home. The dogs saw us and came running. Mamma remarked, "There's no place like home." How true.

As mentioned earlier, we never saw Grandma again. Tuberculosis was a terrible sickness that had existed in the world for hundreds of years. How to treat it exactly was not known, but by the 1940s they began to figure out what to do. When I first started school at Virgil, every student was tested for TB when we were given our childhood shots. A small needle was inserted under the skin on our arm with a form of TB and, if the spot became red and inflamed, it was considered a positive test and further testing would be required.

In the 1920s TB was the fifth most common cause of death. It was sometimes referred to it as consumption or wasting. My grandmother had this illness for a good portion of her life. She had been in the hospital at Norton once prior to our visit, but got well enough to return home to Toronto. When her symptoms worsened again, she went back to the hospital and it was there where she passed away at the age of 66 years in 1951, only six years short of women's life expectancy at the time. Sadly, her quality of life had never been good except during her younger years.

Chapter 17 R̦

The New John Deere

The day was gorgeous, it was mid-morning and the sun was shining bright. The temperature had to be in the high sixties and not a cloud in the sky. I could hear off in the distance the sound of a couple of crows, and then just a few feet to the east above the trees, I could see them soaring, probably looking for dinner or maybe a place to make a nest. We always had a lot of crows around our place, maybe it was because we grew a lot of corn and didn't have a scarecrow either.

It was the spring of 1950. I was just five years old. We were outside and I was helping with the morning chores feeding the pigs, cows, and the bottle calves which was my favorite task when a big truck pulled into the barnyard with a new bright green tractor with yellow wheels on it. Daddy hadn't said anything about it before so I was really surprised. It looked so shiny. The man driving the truck pulled up to where my father was standing and asked where there was a ditch he could back up to and unload. Daddy knew just what he needed so he took him out to the county road a little way toward Virgil, and the man backed the truck around so the truck's back wheels were in the ditch, and then drove the new tractor onto level ground. Then he asked if Daddy wanted to drive the tractor back to the barn and, of course, he said yes. I was excited when Daddy then asked me if I wanted to get up and stand on the platform in front of him. "Sure!" I said.

Just as we were about to get on the road, a beautiful meadow lark took flight. I said, "Daddy, did you see that bird with the big yellow breast? It was the same color as the wheels of our new tractor. So pretty."

The man came back to the barn and had Daddy sign some papers and off he went. As he left, he yelled out his window,

"Enjoy that new tractor." Daddy waved back to him saying, "Thank you."

I excitedly told Daddy we needed to show Mamma. I stood on the platform in front of the driver's seat and Daddy let me do the steering as we very slowly went toward the house.

The new tractor had tricycle-type front tires, and of course made the famous "pop, pop, pop......" that the John Deere tractors were famous for at that time. Mamma had been looking out the front kitchen window and could see us coming. She came out the screen door smiling and commented, "It sure looks pretty." We all looked at each other and just smiled.

I don't think my father had purchased any new equipment since World War II. Daddy had talked about how all the manufacturing had gone into making Army tanks and such instead of farm equipment. Mamma went inside and Daddy and I drove around the barnyard while he taught me how to drive, stop, and even how to put it in the first gear and start the engine.

A few days later, Henry Hanson pulled into the driveway and I yelled my usual, "We got company!" The dogs came out from under one of the hay wagons and Daddy came walking out from the milk barn and over to where Henry had stopped. Henry smiling said, "Howdy, Bill. I hear you got a new tractor." Then Daddy motioned for me to go get it. I took off like I was a cowboy chasing a wild steer, and that was fast.

I got to the barn, checking to see if the brakes were off, and then crawled up behind the steering wheel. I would not have been able to do this with almost any other tractor made at the time, but the John Deere B was special. First, the big steering wheel was placed straight up and down, and secondly. the seat was too high for me to sit on but there was a fairly good-sized platform to stand on. I could reach the throttle so I could set it in the lower range before starting the engine. If the brakes were set, I could just take a wrench and knock them free before starting the tractor.

I began by putting the gearshift into a slot marked 1. Then only two steps remained: starting the tractor by stepping on the starter button (which was on the platform I was standing on), then reaching down and pulling the hand clutch back toward

New John Deere tractor, proud father and happy Robert. cica 1950.

me. Off I went at a snail's pace. It was also good that the tractor had tricycle front wheels so I could see which way to steer
them.

The dogs who had been watching all this activity seemed to
sense danger with me behind the wheel and quickly moved out
of the way. My dad stood with his head tilted back, wearing his
straw hat and a big smile on his face. That reaction from Daddy
gave me a great feeling of confidence and pride since I knew I
was making him proud and happy.

When I reached Daddy and Henry, Henry asked, "Bill, when
will I see Robert out plowing?" We all three laughed and it
made me feel so good to please my father. In addition, I just
felt special standing up on the tractor's platform, driving that
shiny green John Deere with bright yellow wheels. I even forgot
for a few moments about not having a horse, which was very
seldom. The tractor was nice, but in no way took the place of
my wanting my own horse. It would be another year before that
dream came true, so back to riding my stick horse named Trigger, which would have to do for now.

Chapter 18

Grandma's Funeral

It was Thursday, May 3, 1951, a typical spring day. It had been raining and Daddy wasn't able to get into the field to plant corn so he had spent most of the day working on the new hay baler.

I got out of school and talked with my classmates Myrna and Margaret a few minutes before getting on the bus and heading home. Because of the rain, the roads were fairly muddy and we slid around a couple of times before coming to the old black bridge and then on to our place. As usual, the dogs came running to greet us and, of course, because of the rain and mud they made a mess of me. I thought Oh, no. Mamma is not going to love this. Marilyn and I went inside and the screen door slammed behind us. There sat Mamma and Daddy at the kitchen table with very sad looks on their faces.

Daddy told us, "Grandma passed away this morning. Your mother is very upset so we all need to pull together the next couple of days." Marilyn gave Momma a hug and I went over and sat on her lap. All I could say was, "Mamma, I love you." I knew losing her mother really hurt and she felt bad. I knew losing my Mamma would be just about the worst thing that could ever happen to me.

Mamma said, "Now, since you kids are home, I am going to call Frances and tell her what happened. I didn't want to tell her while she was teaching class." I understood that. Because I was one of her students and her brother, I probably would have sensed something was wrong and been upset myself if she had been called out of class. Mamma also told us she had called Freda and Lola earlier in the day.

Daddy went out to do the chores even though it was a little early, and Marilyn told Mamma she would cook dinner. Mamma said, "No, I will fix dinner; I just need to do something to get this off my mind."

Mamma hadn't even noticed how muddy I was or, if she did, she just didn't want to deal with it right then. After changing clothes, I headed to the barn to watch Daddy milk the cows, but just as I was walking out the door, I heard the telephone ring. I kept going as the screen door slammed behind me. I thought about picking up one of my stick horses but thought maybe I was getting too old for that, and I really didn't feel like it anyway. I hoped I would get a real horse of my own sometime soon.

Daddy and I finished doing the chores, but this time Daddy and I fed the chickens so Mamma wouldn't have to. I sure hoped we did it right because those chickens were Mamma's pride and joy. In addition, the baby chicks were in the brooder house and they took special care. During this time, my mind kept going back to the trip we had taken to see Grandma. It had been really fun even though it was extremely hot.

As soon as Daddy and I went into the house, Mamma told us she got a call from Campbell's in Yates Center. "Grandma's body will arrive first thing in the morning and the funeral will be on Sunday with a viewing Saturday afternoon. I need to go to Toronto tomorrow, sometime around noon. I am going to meet my sisters and help with the planning."

Saturday came and we all started taking our baths early. We were later going to be headed toward Toronto for Grandma's visitation that afternoon at the Campbell's Furniture Store on Main Street in downtown Toronto. The Campbells did not have a mortuary in Toronto but used their furniture store for visitations. They kept the body there overnight because the funeral was to be held there the next day. In that time period, it was very common for the body of the deceased to be taken to their home and remain there until it was time for the services but, in Grandma's case, her body was left at the store.

The visitation and viewing started about 3:30 in the afternoon and a large number of people began arriving. As people started going in to see Grandma, a number of them started crying. It affected me and I began to whimper when Mamma said to me, "Big boys don't cry." I was so taken aback, but I wanted to honor Mamma and did not cry; I just wanted to show that I was a big boy, if only six years old.

We finally left and drove home. Daddy hadn't milked the cows yet so he had to do so before we could have a very late supper and go to bed.

The funeral was held on Sunday afternoon, and then Grandma was taken to the Toronto Cemetery where she was laid to rest. A lot of people hung around for a little while before drifting off toward their homes. I had made it the whole day without crying. I felt like I was a grown up and knew Mamma was proud.

The summer of 1951 turned out to be one of the most eventful years of my life, both with disaster and moments of great joy. You could say the year was probably more of a turning point than any other of my entire life, although 1952 would give 1951 a race for the title.

Chapter 19

My Sister Goes to College

It was in the spring of 1950 that my sister Frances graduated from Virgil High School, with the honor of being named valedictorian. I really didn't know what that was but Mamma explained, "It means she is really smart." I wasn't sure what smart was but I assumed it was something good. I hadn't even been to school yet but knew it wouldn't be long.

Mr. Dehlinger, the superintendent of schools, encouraged Frances to go to Emporia State Teachers College. He explained they had a special program, and if she would go to college for two semesters and two summers, they would give her a provisional teaching certificate. She could start teaching immediately and then continue to take classes each summer until she completed the required number of credits for a degree. That meant she could begin teaching in the fall of 1951 before actually becoming a certified teacher in the State of Kansas.

My parents held Mr. Dehlinger in the highest regard and agreed this would be a good career path for Frances to follow. So, the decision was made; Frances was going to college almost immediately. Daddy knew he was going to lose his best tractor driver on the hay baler. Unfortunately, I was too small to fill in, so he gave the opportunity to my sister Marilyn, but that didn't work out so well and he had to hire someone.

The day finally came for Frances to leave for the faraway place called Emporia, and she left on a Saturday morning in early June. I remember the weather was superb. A friend of hers, who also was going to be attending the same college, came by to pick her up. As her ride pulled into the barnyard, the dogs barked and I yelled my customary, "We got company!"

Frances came out of the house carrying a suitcase and a few hanging things. The dogs came nearby, sensing a change was coming. I knew Frances was leaving and I was losing one of my sisters for a while. What I didn't realize was that this would become more permanent than I had thought. She never moved back home, and only visited for a short time now and then. I guess my not knowing was okay because I might have been even more sad than I was.

Mamma and Marilyn came out of the house, and Daddy came from the barn to see Frances off. Everyone seemed to be very happy for her and we all gave her a hug before she got into the car that took her from us. The last thing Mamma said was, "Don't forget to write; I put some stamps in your purse." Then the car pulled away from our farm. We stood there and watched as the car disappeared from view and then Daddy said, "I sure am going to miss her at haying time."

Frances started classes in the summer of 1950 and finally graduated in 1967 after 17 years and hundreds of trips to the college, taking classes wherever and whenever she could find them available. This included most summers. Although it took many years for her to complete the coursework, as promised, Mr. Dehlinger offered her a teaching position in Virgil after she obtained the provisional certificate in the fall of 1951.

I graduated only two years later in 1969 from Wichita State University.

Chapter 20

R̜p

Beginning First Grade

It was the first day of school in 1950, a day I would remember the rest of my life. How excited I was, and a little scared! That day, I would make many new friends and experience many new sights and sounds, and a few new tastes and smells. And, the experiences would be almost boundless after learning my letters and numbers. But I knew I would miss Mamma, the dogs, Mickey (who became my first horse) and my buddy Heifer while I was at school.

A couple days earlier, Mamma had gone to Commons' Store to buy me two new pencils, a box of crayons, and a Big Chief tablet. She had them altogether in a paper sack ready to go.

The morning of the great send-off to school, I got out of bed when it was still dark outside and Daddy had just come in from milking. Rubbing my eyes I went into the kitchen where Mamma had already fixed my coffee, or as my sisters used to call it: "fixing my milk and sugar with a little coffee in it." About that time, the old rooster let out his horrendously loud "cock-a-doodle-doo," and Mamma quipped that "the old boy is running a little late this morning." But he didn't quit his obnoxious crowing until everyone and everything was awake and the sun had peaked over the eastern horizon with a pink glow.

Sister Marilyn stumbled down the stairs and immediately asked if I were ready for this huge happening, and prepared for sitting at a desk all day long. Then she sat down at her place at the breakfast table, serving herself a couple of eggs.

I remember answering, "I guess, but I don't know about sitting all day. Won't they let you go to the outhouse?" Then Marilyn chuckled and said, "only if you are good, maybe." Scowling a little bit, Mamma told her, "Don't tease Robert like that. He is concerned enough already."

Soon, we finished breakfast and I started getting ready, of course, with Mamma's help. She had laid all my clothes out the night before and I just had to put them on. Soon Marilyn walked by and said, "You look pretty good, little brother." WOW! Something nice from my sister! This was starting out to be a rare day.

We were waiting in the kitchen for the bus to come. I was thinking this could be scary, and a very big thing. I knew two of the boys who would be in my class: Raymond Engle and Ronnie Christlieb who were neighbors. One lived just one mile west of us, and the other just one mile south, close to the mailbox. I had the opportunity to spend time with them both, not a lot, but enough to get somewhat acquainted and I felt comfortable being with them.

Marilyn was getting ready to go also. It made me braver knowing she would be going with me. I was starting the first grade and she was just entering her freshman year in high school. I had been to the school before to attend Christmas programs and Vacation Bible school, so I was somewhat familiar with where things were. I knew where the outhouse was which was actually inside, and it even had running water to wash our hands. I didn't understand washing hands every time you went to the outhouse because we didn't have any way to do that at home. Oh well, I thought. I guess they do things different in town. Maybe that is why they are called "city slickers." It didn't take me long to realize that these outhouses were called restrooms. Maybe they would have been better called relief rooms, but I guessed it really didn't matter. A few people called them bathrooms but there wasn't any place to take a bath.

Every day since I was born and school was in session, I had seen my sisters get on the bus and leave for school and return home. They spent a lot of time at school and it all took place in that big wonderful building sitting on top of the hill in town. They seemed to be very excited to go each morning, and when they arrived home in the afternoon, they were laughing and talking in excited voices. They talked about everything—their friends, basketball games, and now and then, boys. Now, it was my time to enjoy the fun in going to school, but a little sadness came over me. Would Mamma miss me or how would it be to be away from her for so long? My young mind was now mixed up. Happy and sad at the same time. How could that be?

When the dogs started barking, Mamma looked out the front window and announced that the school bus was coming. My heart seemed to stop and a lump formed in my throat. The world started spinning. Even though I believed we had thought everything through, I couldn't find my lunch, or even my bag of school supplies. I just stood there paralyzed and I could feel a tear slip out of my eye. Marilyn, being the old pro at going to school, calmly got her things together and walked out with the screen door slamming behind her.

I immediately felt I was being left behind and yelled, "Wait on me!" How could I do this without my sister? Mamma then handed my paper bag of supplies and my lunch to me. I stepped outside and my dog Happy immediately jumped up on me and almost knocked me down.

Mamma was with me and quickly admonished, "Don't let those dogs get you dirty." Oh, no. Again, a reminder about being dirty. Why can't everyone just let me live? After all, a dirty boy was a happy boy.

Before going any farther, Mamma said, "Let me give you a hug." Looking down while hugging me, she saw a little dirt behind by ear. Immediately she reached for her apron and then with a little moisture from her mouth, started rubbing. Was it going to be like this every morning? I wondered why my ears attracted so much dirt.

Marilyn was far ahead of me and was almost at the bus by then. It was big and yellow with windows by each seat except for one which had a broken window and a board where the glass was supposed to be.

The bus pulled close to where we were standing and stopped. All of a sudden, the door flipped open. There sat the driver holding some kind of handle and he told us politely to get in and find ourselves a seat. I noticed the driver's handle was a lever that could open and close the door with just one pull.

I thought, look at all those kids; there must have been hundreds, all talking and laughing at the same time. Is this what school was going to be like? The bus really only had about twenty riders, but it certainly looked like a lot more than that to me.

Marilyn had found a seat and saved part of it for me for which I was very thankful. For some reason, I thought she would have rather been sitting with one of her friends, but as a big sister, she had responsibilities and that was me. Mamma would have been very unhappy if she hadn't watched out for me, and I knew it. So, I confessed, "Marilyn, I feel a little scared right now." She put her arm around me and gave me a hug. She then promised, "I will take you into your classroom to meet your teacher once we get there."

The bus was now pulling out of the driveway and it shook, rattled and dust went everywhere. Then the noise level rose around me. I guessed this is what a bunch of kids do when they get together—make a lot of noise. It was somewhat intimidating for me and caused me to be uncomfortable. But it wouldn't take long before I would become one of those noisy youngsters.

We soon came to the corner where we turned east, and after a short distance, the bus made a diagonal turn to the south. And there it was—the old black bridge! I suddenly realized I was going to have to cross that thing every day going back and forth to school. The bus slowed down and stopped for another car that was approaching from the other side. After the car crossed, we then proceeded on.

The front wheels went bump onto the wooden deck of the bridge and that old thing once again started to shake, squeak, swing, rattle, and sway. Being high up in the bus looking out I was startled that I could see down into the river. It was really a long way down there and a view that I hadn't seen from our car. There wasn't much water but it seemed to have a lot of driftwood, and even a couple of 55-gallon drums along with quite a few glass bottles that all made it look kind of trashy. Finally, the bus pulled off onto the road on the other side. I had survived!

In just a few minutes, we pulled up in front of the huge building, the one I could see all the way from our house. There were many more kids, and even some grownups coming to the school. The bus driver pulled on the lever and like magic, the door opened again. The driver said, "Be careful." Everyone stood up and we started toward the door.

Marilyn took a hold of my hand, which felt very reassuring. I was a big boy and was a little reluctant to have my sister hold

Virgil School, both grade and high school.

my hand but, in this case, it really gave me some confidence. We went into the school and I think my sister knew everyone because she said hello to them all.

Then she said, "Robert, over here is your room. I will take you in and introduce you to your teacher, and then you are on your own." We turned and went into a great big room with huge windows and lots of desks and a lady quickly stepped up and said, "I bet you are Robert. My name is Miss Lewis."

Now how did she know my name? I wondered. I hadn't seen her before. But WOW! She was just down-right pretty too, kind of small with the most wonderful eyes and beautiful red hair. I knew then school was going to be a wonderful thing. I was immediately in love and had no idea what love was, but I was in it and it felt good.

Marilyn let go of my hand and told me she would see me after school. Before leaving, she touched me on the head as if to say "that everything will be okay."

Miss Lewis led me over to a desk and said, "This one is for you, Robert. You sit here until school starts; it won't be long." People kept bringing more students into the classroom, leaving them with Miss Lewis. Shortly after, the loudest bell I had ever heard went off, and my heart jumped into my throat. I soon learned this bell was a love-hate bell. You always hated it when it meant it was time to sit down and start working, but loved it when it was time for recess, dinner, or time to go home.

After the bell sounded, Miss Lewis went to the front of the room and explained how happy she was to meet us all and what a wonderful year we were going to have. She also explained that if we needed to go number one, we were to hold up one finger, and if number two, two fingers. It didn't take me long to figure out what one finger or two fingers meant. After all, I was a farm boy and not stupid, although there was still some confusion. Why didn't we just hold up our hand since we were going to the same place anyway? Oh well, I was sure there would be other things I didn't understand.

Looking around the room there was a picture of an older man who had white hair, but the picture didn't show his whole body. It hung on the wall and looked like it had been there for a long time. I noticed too that the room had very high ceilings, almost like our barn. There were tall windows on two sides of the room with white blinds. I found out later that the picture was of someone known as Washington and had to do with history a long time ago. I thought he must be really important because at home, we only had one picture. That was of Jesus and I knew he was important.

Still standing at the front of the class, Miss Lewis explained we would say the Pledge of Allegiance to the Flag and the Lord's Prayer each day. She then asked us to stand up, facing the flag, and put our right hand over our hearts and repeat after her, the Pledge of Allegiance. That was the first time I knew my heart was on the left side. I also learned which side was my left. Next, with everyone still standing, she directed us to say the Lord's Prayer. Afterwards, she told us some might feel better saying a couple of things different in the prayer which I did not understand. I would be lucky to just get anything out of my mouth.

This room held the first and second grades. Since Miss Lewis would be teaching both classes at the same time, I thought she must be really smart. We were instructed to put our Big Chief tablets, pencils and crayons into our desks. Letting my hands run all over my desk top, side and underneath, I soon found that someone had stuck old chewing gum under it, and there were lots of it. I guessed that is how to get rid of the gum if you needed to because Miss Lewis explained that chewing gum in class was not allowed. Just maybe that resulted in lots of gum where it wasn't supposed to be, like under desks.

She handed out some sheets of paper with lines drawn on them, and we were told to start practice writing a,b,c,d,e and f. If we needed help, we were to look up at the top of the blackboard, where all the letters were, to see how they were made. We wrote the letters again and again while Miss Lewis went to the class side with the second graders to talk with them.

It wasn't long before I was tired of writing letters when Miss Lewis said, "Now you are going to learn how to write your names." She showed each one of us how to do our name, and then we practiced it time and time again. I soon discovered that doing something until you got really tired of it was the way we were going to learn, and it would be boring. I also learned really quickly that some of the students had probably cheated because they knew how to write their letters before they even came to school. But the next thing I learned was more astonishing—the girls were smarter than boys. This was very disappointing. After all, my sisters didn't seem that smart.

Next, Miss Lewis handed a book to each one of us (maybe the most important book we would study) titled *Dick and Jane.* We were told that this was a new way to teach reading. The explanation given was as follows: In the classroom, phonics drills of letter sounds are replaced by word flashcards. The teacher holds up cards with "house," "up," "down," or "Spot" written out, and the students practice recognizing the word.

I must say I had no idea what my teacher was trying to tell us about this new system. What I didn't know then was that reading would be the most important thing I would learn, and how well I did in school and life depended on my reading skills. Which turned out to not be very good, or better said, terrible. All my life I have struggled with reading and comprehension.

Before long, it was time to go home. The loud bell went off again—the happy bell. When we started to leave, Miss Lewis's parting words were, "See you tomorrow." When we got on the bus to go home, I sat with Raymond Ingle. I no longer needed the comfort of my sister; I had grown up a lot in that one day. I learned how to write my name, ate my sack lunch and drank the milk they provided at school. There must have been something wrong with the milk, it just had a different taste. Maybe it didn't come from a cow, but maybe somewhere else...like a goat? I couldn't wait to get home to see Mamma and tell her all about the first day, pet my dogs and hug Heifer.

The bus was off, rattling as it always did, and soon it came to that old black bridge, crossed it, and finally we made it home. When the bus let Marilyn and me off, we both went running to the house. The dogs had barked when the bus pulled in so Mamma was standing at the door waiting on us, wiping her hands on her apron. I couldn't wait to tell her I could write my name. We went inside where Mamma had fixed a jelly sandwich for me with a big glass of real cow's milk.

Daddy did the chores and brought the milk in for separating while Mamma got supper ready. I remember that it was ham and beans with corn bread, one of my favorites. Of course, I had to add ketchup to my beans as I added ketchup to almost everything. We ate and talked a long time, just sitting there, even after we had finished supper.

The talk was all about the first day of school. Proudly I announced, "I can write my name." As soon as I found a pencil and paper, I began showing off my new skill. They could tell I still needed a whole lot of practice, but they acted very impressed. Then I said, "At dinner time they gave us the most terrible tasting milk. I really want milk that comes from cows." Mamma chuckled and explained to me that their milk was pasteurized. She tried to explain that they had to cook it to kill the bacteria. Throughout the next few weeks, I finally got to where I could tolerate the milk, and even started to like it.

We finally got ready for bed. Mamma looked at me and commented that, "You sure look tired. School is a lot of work, isn't it?" Rubbing my eyes, I readily agreed. I lay down and, before I went to sleep, I could hear a coyote or two. I guess I was fairly exhausted because it seemed it wasn't long before I was waking up by hearing Daddy come in from milking and the crowing of the old rooster.

The next morning everything went like it was supposed to in getting ready for school. Even the dogs seemed to know there was a new routine taking place here at the farm. They quickly learned when I came outside, it was to go to school and not to play with them. This was serious stuff now. I think my mother must have had a talk with them about keeping me clean. After all, I was making new friends, and for sure didn't want Miss Lewis thinking I was a dirty little boy. I wanted to be a good student like I am sure my sisters had been, especially since my sister Frances was the valedictorian of her senior class last year (1950). I remembered Mamma told me that this was a big honor.

The bus came and I ran, leaving my sister behind. I jumped on and immediately went to sit by Raymond. Marilyn got on and the bus took off. Before long we were crossing that old black bridge and arriving at school. I then remembered I had not given Mamma a hug before running to the bus. I felt bad.

This day was a whole lot like the day before and Miss Lewis

was still beautiful. When the bell rang, we all sat down and then stood up again to say the Lord's Prayer and the Pledge of Allegiance. After that, we sat down and started practicing writing our letters again and again.

A few minutes later, a very loud clinking noise started that just scared me to death. Miss Lewis told us, "This is a fire drill. You all need to stand up and get into a line so we can walk out together."

I thought if there is a fire, we need to get out of here fast. I had noted when Daddy burned the pasture, it was extremely hot. I apparently hadn't heard the word drill or didn't understand what it meant because after standing up, I grabbed the paper I was working on and we walked out of our classroom in a single file. When we were outside waiting to go back into the building, someone laughingly asked me why I brought my paper. I simply said, "If the school house burns down, I don't want to have to do all that work over again." The rest of the day went along well and before I knew it, we were crossing that old black bridge on the way home.

That evening at the dinner table, I asked Daddy to tell me about when he went to school. He looked up, scratched his ear and looking directly at me jokingly said, "Son, I only went to the third grade. By that time, I knew I had learned all I could and that I was smarter than the teachers." We all laughed.

Still, I was amazed and replied that he must be really smart. Then he further explained, "Son, school seemed to come hard for me, and I always would have much rather been outside working in the fields with the horses." He went on to say they were tenant farmers on a very poor farm, and he was needed at home to help, just so the family would survive.

Then Mamma, as she started to stack the dinner dishes interjected, "Robert, let me tell you about when I went to school. We lived about two miles from the school in the Carlisle neighborhood south of Toronto. We had to walk, and had no school bus. Then after grade school I wanted to go to high school. It was in Toronto proper, about eight miles away. I rode a horse to town on Sunday afternoon and stayed with one of my mother's aunts during the week, and on Friday afternoon, I rode back home. They had a place for me to keep the horse in Toronto and I was very grateful to be able to go to school. My other three sisters didn't have this privilege and seemed to resent that fact. I got a teaching job immediately out of high school."

I asked, "Mamma why are you not a teacher anymore?"

Then she replied, "Well, I met your father who lived just down the road from our place. We fell in love and got married, and married women were not allowed to be teachers as it is still today."

I voiced my strong opinion, "That's not fair!"

After starting to get a grasp of writing and a little reading, I decided it was time to venture out and start using these new skills. Now it was time to write my first letter, a very big step in my professional development. Failure would mean a big setback to me, not to mention a major blow to my ego. So, failure was not an acceptable option. When I had a major problem, I consulted Mamma and not a sister. They just can't be trusted in important situations like this.

Chapter 21

R_P

First Letter

Because of the high cost of long-distance telephone calls, we almost never made one, so writing letters was very important, and my mother keeping in touch with her family was, likewise, very important to her. Before starting school, I saw her writing letters for what seemed to be hours to her mother, her sisters and brothers and, of course, her daughters. Then when a letter came in return from anyone, she was very excited and happy to get news from them.

When Frances went to college, it seemed like Mamma's letter writing went into overdrive. I was happy now that I was learning my letters and how to write my name. I was sure, with a little help from Mamma, I could write a letter to Frances too. This would be my first big challenge in using my newly learned skills. I was sure that I was becoming smarter now and wanted to begin using some of my education. In the end, I didn't want it to go to waste.

Mamma and I sat down at the kitchen table with paper and pencil. She asked what I wanted to write to Frances and my mind went completely blank. It was almost like when you want to write a book, where do you start? Mamma suggested thinking of something that was going on in my life. I started off, of course, with "Dear Frances" and wrote about going over to some of our friends the next day, and then about one of our cows having a calf. I ended the letter by writing: "I would like to see my Heifer. I never do." I signed the letter, "Robert."

This letter expressed what was on my mind, including the sadness I had because I hadn't seen my cow Heifer. She had been put out with the other cows in the north pasture.

Writing was exciting to me because I was using something I had learned in school. I did have a lot of help from Mamma.

I know I could not have spelled any of the words except my name, Robert.

My letter went in the envelope with the one from Mamma and we took it to the mailbox, about a mile from our place. We put up the red flag to tell the rural mail carrier, Bud Fisher, that a letter was inside and to please stop and pick it up. The postage was only three cents, a real bargain compared to today at a rate of seventy-three cents.

This was almost as exciting as the first day of school. I had now used some of my new knowledge to communicate with my sister. I thought maybe someday I will even use my numbers to count my money...if I ever have any.

The days went by and everything settled into a routine. I loved going to school each day and seeing Miss Lewis since she was so pretty. I told my sister I was in love with her. Then Marilyn informed me that Miss Lewis was getting married in December, just a couple of months away. That broke my heart. Now I have had two love disappointments in my young life! First, I had fallen for Dale Evans to only be told she was married to Roy Rogers, and now Miss Lewis was going to get married. Her name was changing and we would have to call her Mrs. Cannon. I wondered what happened if I forgot and called her Miss Lewis; maybe I would be in trouble. This changing name thing was going to be real confusing, but I guess since I had only known her for a couple of months, it shouldn't be too bad.

Marilyn suggested that I look for a younger girl in my class. So, the hunt was on. It didn't take long; sitting in the desk next to me was a little petite girl with bright eyes, big smile, and beautiful hair who spoke in a soft voice. Her name was Myrna Pennebaker. I started talking with her a lot and then holding her hand. Wow! This was what having a girlfriend was all about, I was sure. Soon, we even kissed. Then my world just crashed.

Miss Lewis talked to both of us, saying it was not proper for children of our age to carry on as such. Dang. There goes another girlfriend. We had seen some of those high school boys and girls doing this. Maybe they weren't supposed to be doing it either but they didn't listen to their teachers. I didn't know what to think. We were embarrassed. I guess to have a girlfriend you had to go undercover. But Myrna and I went our separate ways, and it would be eight more years before I got up enough courage to kiss another girl. Naturally, sisters don't count. Anyway, who would want to kiss his sister?

One of the things that I enjoyed so much was the period right after dinner when Miss Lewis would read us a chapter out of a book. The book that I liked most was a story about a family living in the colonial days, back in the New England area. The little boy of the family was given the job of training the baby oxen, starting just a few days after the baby bull calves were born. I could relate to this after playing with my calf Heifer. I never taught her anything other than how to lead but we were a team. She would let me lead her anywhere, never giving me trouble, and seemed to enjoy our friendship. She would lean up next to me and I would pet her.

This story, read to our class in the first grade by Miss Lewis, made such an impression on me that in later life it led me to purchase a pair of bull calves when they were only five or six days old. I bottle fed them and trained them on how to work as a team, wearing a small ox yoke. I find it very interesting that something read to me in 1950 in the first grade, could motivate me to take action on it forty-five years later.

One day, a man whom I had seen around the school, looking very professional and dignified, wearing a white shirt with long sleeves and a colorful neck tie, came into our classroom. Miss Lewis introduced him as Mr. Dehlinger. He told us we were going down to the gymnasium and get some exercise. I didn't understand why we would need exercise because I was always running, jumping, getting away from the dogs and, of course, climbing. But, maybe this would be fun. He had us get into a single file line and follow him.

We went to the gym and played some games, most of which involved a good-sized ball filled with air. He threw it, caught it, and even bounced it on the floor. It had turned out to be a lot of fun and I hoped we would get to do it again soon.

Years later talking with Sam Robison and telling him about the first time I ever met Mr. Dehlinger, Sam asked if I knew what he was doing. I assumed just getting to know the first and second graders. Sam emphatically said, "No. He was scouting his upcoming prospects for future basketball teams." Coach was always looking forward to when he would have a state basketball championship. Maybe our class was the one which would bring it to Virgil for him.

Before long, it was the afternoon before Thanksgiving and Marilyn and I had already gotten home from school when my sister Frances came home from college. She was riding with a friend and, when they pulled into the barnyard, the dogs went to greet them and I yelled, "Frances is home!" She got out of the car and I helped her to carry in her things, hoping she had brought me something. Then Mamma came to the door with a big smile, and wiping her hands on her apron, said she was really glad Frances was home and was looking forward to hearing all about college.

Daddy, who was working in the barn, walked up to the house to also welcome Frances home. We were all smiles, even the dogs. Daddy soon left to go back to his work, but I just wanted to be there with Frances, Marilyn and Mamma. They talked and talked, and I was hardly able to get a question in or given the opportunity to tell her about my school. I wanted to so much tell her about my writing skills. Finally I gave up, but then realized I had sent her a letter along with one of Mamma's, so she knew already I could write. Then I headed outside to the barn to be with Daddy.

That evening at supper, Mamma fixed some fried calves' liver and onions, one of Frances and Daddy's favorite, in addition to stewed tomatoes, green beans, mashed potatoes and gravy, corn bread and a raisin pie. That was a treat; I thought it must have been special because Frances was home.

The next day was Thanksgiving. Our family was not real big on celebrating the holiday. It was kind of like a Sunday but, if there was work to be done, we just went about doing it.

Frances told me that in earlier years, Daddy and Mamma would go to the cornfield to pick corn on Thanksgiving. If it was cold outside, Mamma put on one of Daddy's pair of overalls to keep warm. Although, Mamma told me that if it was extremely cold, Daddy would take a bunch of cornstalks and build a fire so she could get a little warmer. This being the days when the wagon was pulled by horses and the corn was picked by hand.

Frances also told me that Mamma picked the row next to the wagon, and Daddy picked rows two and three. The horses were trained well enough that when it came time for the wagon to be pulled up, all Daddy had to do was just say to the team, "Step up, step up," until they moved forward as far as he wanted the wagon moved. Then he would say, "Whoa."

This particular Thanksgiving, there was no corn to be picked and the workhorses were no longer on our farm. We just had a normal dinner. Both Frances and Marilyn left to be with friends, and I was on my own to just be a little boy around the farm, but I knew how to keep myself busy. Unfortunately, this just keeping busy would also sometimes get me into trouble. Like the time I took the paintbrush from inside the bucket of grease and proceeded to paint everything in the barn with it. Daddy was not amused and I even got a whipping.

When the weekend was finally over, Frances left to go back to Emporia for college and Marilyn and I got ready to go back to school. It wouldn't be long before Frances would be home again for Christmas break. I could hardly wait since that would be almost two whole weeks.

Chapter 22

First Christmas with Electric Lights

It was 1950 and I was very excited for Christmas to get here, although I had one major worry: How could Santa get into our house? We did not have a fireplace. Instead, we had a potbelly stove and only a pipe came through the ceiling and into it. I fretted and worried about this for weeks. I guess that I hadn't thought about how he got inside the previous years. This was just a new thing for me to worry about.

Eventually, I brought the subject up with my sister Marilyn, explaining to her my fears. She said, "I think what you should be worrying about is whether or not you have been a good boy this year, silly boy. You know we never lock the backdoor, and in fact there is not even a lock on it."

Oh no! Another thing to fret about, and maybe it was even a little too late to worry about my past year's behavior. I took a short inventory. I hadn't thrown any rocks at the chickens, at least that anybody knew of. I never got sent to the principal's office at school but Miss Lewis had scolded me just a few times. Surely it wasn't bad to say, "sic'em" to the dogs so they would chase the cats. Even Daddy did that. How about that time I stuck my gum under my desk at school, or when I complained about my sisters and really shouldn't have? Then again, I only used bad words once or twice, and that was when they were really needed. Not getting my ears clean didn't count, did it? If by chance there really was no way I could expect anything from Santa, I think Mamma would tell him to overlook most of my shortcomings. At least I hoped so.

That night when I went to bed, I had a hard time going to sleep. I don't know if it was because of all the coyotes that kept yipping or maybe just thinking about all the bad things I may have done. The last thing I heard was one of the old cows down at the barn, mooing as if to be looking for her baby calf.

Anxiety aside, what was really most exciting to me was that this would be the first Christmas we were going to have electricity. That, in itself, was almost a great present. Now, with that big light on the pole, I could go outside in the dark and not be too scared. That is, if I didn't go out too far.

The next most exciting thing was that we could now have electric Christmas lights on our tree for the first time. Hurrah! I just wanted to jump up and down with joy. This was something those kids in town had, and an experience I never had before. I realized I could now even be gifted an electric train! That was special. When I was four years old, Santa brought me a wind-up train, but it meant spending most of my time just winding.

The day finally came to set up the tree. I knew this was going to be fun. Daddy had gone into the pasture and cut down one of the best-looking cedar trees he could find. And while still outside, he put a wooden base on it. Just a day or two earlier, Mamma had been to the Commons' Store to get the strings of electric lights so all was ready.

After preparing the tree to come inside, Daddy set it where the Christmas tree was always placed each year. Luckily, an electrical plug was right there. Marilyn and Mamma got the Christmas decorations, and we were ready. They let me put the first decoration on the tree—one of the rounds, a very shiny red ball. After admiring my work, Mamma said, "Let's put the electric lights on now." As Marilyn and Mamma were putting them on, Marilyn suddenly said, "I see a bird's nest in the tree!" After a little discussion, it was decided to just leave it there.

I couldn't wait to see the electric lights come on; I begged Mamma to plug them in. Wow! They were beautiful and just what I expected. There weren't many lights for this size of tree, but we had real lights and I was super happy. After admiring our beautiful, shining icon, Mamma announced, "Now, Marilyn, you and Robert finish the tree." We started hanging the other decorations. First were the chains of paper loops, red and white made by Frances and Marilyn years prior when they were in grade school. Then came silver icicles and we had a lot of them. We finally finished and yelled for Mamma to come take a look. I specifically pointed out to her what I had put on. She said smiling, "This is the best Christmas tree I have ever seen." The tree smelled good but it was very prickly and somewhat difficult to put things on it, but we got it done.

Over the next day or so, I was really careful not to do anything bad. I even spent a little extra time washing my ears. Frances would be coming home from college in just a couple days so I also decided to be extra nice to my sisters, at least until Christmas was over. And I hoped they would reciprocate.

During the next few days, presents started showing up under the tree. There were even one or two for me which I eagerly noticed since I was now in the first grade and could read, at least my name.

Finally, Frances arrived home and we were all together now. It seemed like Mamma and she would sit in the kitchen for hours just talking. I think Mamma had really missed her, and there was no doubt that Frances was super happy to be home. I didn't even mind they didn't pay as much attention to me; the weather hadn't been really cold so I spent some time outside when I wasn't in school.

I was very excited when I had only one day of school left before Christmas vacation because we had earlier drawn names for a gift exchange. I really don't remember whose name I got, but I remember Mamma had gone to the store to get a gift for me to give. The last day was only a half-day. We exchanged gifts that morning and someone brought cookies so we had a Christmas party. That I can recall, but not what gift I received.

Marilyn and I got on the bus, and before long we were crossing the old black bridge. Arriving home, we stepped off of the bus with the dogs coming to greet us as usual, and then Frances came out of the house. It was so wonderful to have her home! I could see that Frances and Marilyn also had a very close relationship. They had grown up as little girls, almost inseparable. They were only three years apart and they spent six years together before I was born.

We three went inside together, but on the way, I saw a cat coming across the road. I didn't even think but said my usual, "sic'em," to urge the dogs to chase the cat. And then I realized I maybe shouldn't have done that. Oh, well, maybe Santa's busy making toys and missed what I did. It was really hard to be good all of the time.

Later, when Mamma had supper ready, Daddy came inside after milking the cows. Mamma fixed some potato soup which I really didn't like. I ate a little and asked her to make me a peanut butter and jelly sandwich. As we sat around the dinner table everybody talked a lot, even me. It was so great to have us all together. Frances talked about what was going on at college. Marilyn talked about how the basketball team had been doing, and Mamma talked about news she heard from Wilma Aeschliman and Mrs. Commons. Daddy talked about how his calves were doing along with the hogs, and I talked about how much I had learned in school, including how to write my name, reading *Dick and Jane* and adding numbers.

Finally, Mamma said, "Robert, I need you to get ready for bed," and I countered with, "Mamma, can we leave the Christmas lights on tonight?" The answer came back as a resounding, "No!" I later learned it had something to do with fire danger. She tucked me in and said good night along with a kiss. Frances also came over to me and even gave me a kiss too. That was unexpected, and I hoped she was feeling okay. Because I was really tired, I went to sleep almost immediately. I don't think I even heard one coyote.

Before long, it was Christmas Eve. Waiting was almost impossible, but I made it. That night we had oyster soup and I didn't like it either. I think my sisters did, so maybe Mamma was making it for them. I really needed another peanut butter and jelly sandwich. Mamma said, "Robert, once we get cleaned up here, I will help you put up your stocking." We always took one of Daddy's big socks and tied it to a chair brought in from the kitchen to set by the tree, hoping for some gifts.

Afterwards, the coyotes went crazy—howling, yipping and carrying on. Now I was sure that I would never get to sleep and Santa wouldn't come. I was very afraid he might just pass me by this year. Those were my last thoughts and I didn't even realize I'd fallen asleep when suddenly, I was awakened by hearing the backdoor open and the screen close. I didn't know what to do. Was that Santa or was it Daddy coming in from milking? Listening carefully, I heard Daddy say, "Has Robert gotten up yet?"

I yelled, "I'm getting up now," and looked over at the chair with my stocking on it. The stocking was full of candy with an orange in the toe of it. Beside it was a Red Rider BB gun with a switch lying beside it. I yelled, "Whoopee!" Daddy and Mamma came into the living room where I was and said, "Let us see what Santa brought you." I said, "What is the switch for?" and Daddy said, "That is just a reminder of what you might have gotten if you weren't good, but you made it another year."

This was unbelievable; I had really gotten a BB gun and it was even a Red Rider—the same one as in the Montgomery Ward catalog. It was a real beauty. I guess, I hadn't been that bad after all.

"I am going outside right now and see how good my gun works."

Then I heard Mamma say, "Not until you've gotten dressed and had your breakfast."

We suddenly heard the two-sleeping beauties, my sisters, come down the stairs. When I saw them, I said in the most excited voice, "See what I got!" Simultaneously they both replied, "You have to be kidding me." Looking back, I think they thought our parents had gone off the deep end in buying a BB gun for me.

After gifts were opened, we went into the kitchen for breakfast. Mamma poured my coffee and put the cream and sugar in it. Frances acted surprised and asked, "Are you still getting his coffee for him every morning?" I answered before Mamma, "She loves me."

Mamma ignored the question and directed her attention to what she knew would be next on the agenda. "Robert, now I don't want to see you shooting any of my chickens or I will take that thing away from you."

"No, Mamma, I wouldn't do that."

Mamma fixed a big breakfast with eggs, bacon, and pancakes along with a bowl of home-canned peaches. We sat there for a long time talking even though I wanted to get outside and do some shooting. Finally, Daddy spoke up and said, "Robert, I will go outside with you later to give you instructions on shooting. You have to listen and follow my instructions or I will take the gun away until you learn to listen."

Daddy and I did finally go outside for a short time before dinner was ready around noon. It was a baked chicken, and I had to ask, "Mamma, is this that old rooster?" We had joked about making a meal out of him after hearing him crow so loudly all the time. She assured me it was just one of our "old hens."

We, in addition, had mashed potatoes and gravy, cranberry sauce, stuffing, different kinds of pickles and pickled tongue. Then there were both rolls and cornbread muffins along with honey. For dessert, Mamma made a big apple pie.

That afternoon Daddy and I went out for some more shooting, mostly at a can. I think Daddy was having as much fun as I was because he took more turns than I got. The day was finally coming to an end and I never was tempted to shoot at one of Mamma's chickens, even though one of them almost got in the way.

Before getting into bed that night, I shined my Red Rider BB gun and placed it standing up by the door. You never know when you might be attacked by coyotes. Still, I never heard even one coyote. Evidently the word was out that I was now armed.

Years later I came across an old advertisement for the Red Rider BB gun and the recommended age for the gun was between ten and twelve years. I guess my parents thought at six years old, I was very grown up for my age. After all, I could drive the John Deere tractor.

Chapter 23

R
P

Mickey the Horse

I wanted only one thing as much as to be a cowboy; it was having my own horse. My parents had wanted to get one for me and had bought at least one horse that just didn't work out. My father had purchased a dark brown mare and brought her home, but once he saddled and then mounted her, he knew immediately this wasn't the right horse for me. He did decide, however, to keep her around for himself to ride.

The mare was so hard to catch that Daddy attached a light twenty-foot chain to her halter and, even then, she had to be approached very quietly and slowly. One day when I was in the pasture, I was able to get a hold on her. Then I tied her up to a tree and proudly went to tell my father of the catch. But I still wanted my own horse. I did not want just any horse, and especially not one of those Holstein colored ones (also known as a paint). It had to be a palomino like Roy Rogers' Trigger.

Then the day came during the spring of 1951 and the Grub family was having a farm sale, and included was a horse that Carol Grub was selling. I couldn't wait until Saturday came.

My father, I, and my sister Marilyn went to the sale. Daddy had put his saddle and bridle in the car just in case a purchase might be made. When we arrived, I saw one of my classmates from school, Ronnie Christlieb. We said "Hi" to each other and then went our separate ways. Shortly thereafter, the auctioneer started barking out his instructions and explained in what order the items were going to be offered. As everyone was getting ready for the sale, he stated, "We really have a lot of great things. Don't miss out on some of these bargains. Plus, we have one of the best kid ponies in the county for sale here today."

The auctioneer moved up one row of farm equipment and down another of miscellaneous items which included barbwire stretchers, old milk cans, a cream separator, buckets, and log chains. And then it was announced that it was time to sell the horse—the most beautiful horse I had ever seen. It was a paint and already had a name—Mickey. I completely forgot about wanting a palomino.

The bidding went very fast and then it narrowed down to only two bidders: my father and Ronnie Christlieb's dad. The bidding continued and it went quickly over one hundred dollars, but didn't stop there. Soon it was at one hundred and fifty dollars and continued rising even though the bidding seemed to slow down. Finally, it reached two hundred dollars when the bidding seemed to stop and Daddy didn't have the bid. The auctioneer said, "Do I hear two hundred and five?" No response came and the auctioneer said, "This is the last time. Do I hear two hundred and five dollars?" and then my father raised his hand. No other bid came forward and the auctioneer said, "Sold to the man with the young smiling boy." I had finally gotten my own horse! My smile could not have been bigger and, in fact someone said, "That little boy would have broken his face if he smiled anymore."

Someone in the crowd said that's a lot of money for a kid's horse. I am sure Daddy was thinking the same thing, but oh, how happy I was! Daddy then asked if I wanted to ride her home and, of course, I said yes. Since we had brought the saddle and bridle with us, we were prepared. The plan was for six-year-old me and my 14-year-old sister to ride Mickey home.

We had only gone about three miles when Daddy pulled up in the family car and asked how we were doing. I said, "great" but Marilyn said, "I am sun-burnt and very tired." Mickey did not have horse shoes on and the gravel road made her feet become very tender. It just so happened that Daddy had the homemade two-wheel trailer attached to the car. Mickey was loaded onto the platform and we were on our way, with dust boiling out from under the back of the trailer.

Once we made it home, I couldn't wait to show my mother. Mamma watched as we unloaded Mickey and Daddy helped me up into the saddle. I trotted off showing Mamma just how good of a rider I was already. I rode back to where Mamma was

Mickey, Robert, Niece Judy and girl at rear name lost to history.

standing and jumped down to give her a hug. I was so happy. Mamma understood but said, "Robert, now you have to be careful; we don't need any broken arms or something worse."

It is believed that Daddy and Mamma had a talk about the cost of the horse. But if they did, I was never told of the discussion.

I spent the rest of the summer riding and riding and more riding, and never once did I think about Mickey not being a palomino like Roy Rogers' Trigger. She was so tall I could not get on her without a saddle or other means of climbing on. Since Daddy was usually in the field, and no one else could put the saddle on, I had to become very creative in how I could get on Mickey.

The barnyard was easy for me to climb up on Mickey because there was always a hay wagon to get on and jump aboard. The challenges came in other locations, especially the pasture. If Mickey was in the middle of the pasture, I had to lead her to the barbwire fence. The barbwire presented a real problem in climbing the wires, balancing on a fence post, and keeping Mickey close enough to jump on. No little task. Another option in the pasture was to find an eroded area where there was a bank of dirt about horseback height. The problem was getting Mickey to stand still long enough for me to get up there and jump on. This hardly ever worked. In the timber I even tried climbing a tree. As a rule, it was just better to stay on and not get off again.

After starting this book, I was able to visit with Carol (Grub) McKenize at one of the Virgil gatherings. She told me that she really didn't want to sell Mickey but, since they were moving into town, there was no choice. I believe I could still see a little sadness in her eyes all these years later.

Chapter 24

1951 Flood

It was July of 1951 and I seemed to be on top of the world. I had just gotten my dream horse the previous May, electricity had come to our farm, we had gotten a new John Deere tractor, and I had passed the first grade. Life couldn't be any better.

Then it started to rain, in fact, it had rained so much my father was having a hard time getting the corn crop in the ground and the hay crop out of the field. Rain, rain, and it rained some more. It rained so much that my time riding Mickey was being limited. Mamma just wouldn't let me go riding if it looked cloudy and could possibly rain like it did most of the time.

It had been a miserable day and not fun to be outside. I spent most of my time in the barn playing with a new litter of kittens. The mother cat had them on top of a baled hay stacked near the peak of the barn, a safe place far away from where the dogs couldn't get to them. There were four kittens—one black, two black-and-white spotted that resembled the mother cat, and one yellow calico. The kittens were all rolled up in a ball keeping each other warm. They were old enough that their eyes had just opened and were so cute and loving. I liked picking them up and holding them close to my face. What warm, sweet creatures they were!

I loved the kittens when they were so small because, when they were a little older, the mamma cat and her babies would make their way to the milk barn where they'd learn from their mother how to hunt mice. Next, it was on to the timber to continue their training of bug eating and other rodent harvesting.

Suddenly, I could hear my father in the distance calling for me, and I went running to see want he needed. "Daddy, what do you want?"

"Help me get these cows in for milking."

The cow lot was a real mess with mud and manure almost

over the top of my shoes. The cows were standing at the far end, but they headed for the barn once they saw me coming. The cows went right into their stalls splashing water, manure and mud everywhere including on my clothes and in my face, and once, even into my mouth. Yuk! No matter how much I tried to spit and clear my mouth, the taste was still there. Yuk!

Looking at what a mess I was, my father reminded me that I needed to take my clothes off on the back porch when we got to the house. Since it was so terribly muddy, the cows' utters were covered with mud and it was taking Daddy longer than usual to clean them so he could finish milking. He finally told me to run up to the house and tell Mamma we were running late, which I immediately did.

Daddy finally finished and we made our way toward the house. It was still daylight and you could see the sun on the western horizon peeking through the clouds. That was a site we hadn't seen much that spring and summer. But still, just seeing the sun spreading its rays over the Flint Hills to the west made me feel good and a little warmer.

When it rained every day, it felt cold all the time. A person would just want to find a warm place out of the wind, like in the top of the barn playing with the kittens. A nap would feel good to me now on days like that, but then I was a young boy, and there was no time for a nap. What a waste.

Daddy carried the two buckets of milk and I followed along with the three dogs trailing while biting at each other in a playful manner and jumping around and acting silly. They made me smile. Suddenly, a rabbit that had made its way into the barnyard, jumped up and began running, with the dogs chasing after it. I yelled, "Get him," but it was a real race and the rabbit won. The dogs came walking back with their tongues hanging out and wagging their tails. The look of defeat was on their faces. Of course, the dogs never won chases like these so they were used to the feeling of defeat.

The dogs always knew something to eat would be coming soon in the form of supper scraps. We never fed our dogs any store-bought food nor did they ever see a veterinarian. Basically, it was the same for the cats; they were only fed fresh milk at milking time and relied on mice caught in the barn plus other wild life such as birds, grasshoppers and small rodents. Like our livestock, the cats were never named and never brought into the house.

When we reached the door to the back porch, I opened it so Daddy could go straight in, and the screen door slammed behind us. After setting the milk down beside the cream separator, we took our boots off before going inside the house. The dogs stayed outdoors since they were never allowed inside, but that didn't keep them from standing there looking with forlorn expressions on their faces as if to say, "Just once."

Daddy and I washed up in a pan of water Mamma had set on the washstand for us. After throwing the dirty water outside, we went in and Mamma asked Daddy to turn the light on. Daddy reached up and pulled the string on the light in the center of the room. This was a great convenience not having to get matches to light the old kerosene lamp like we had to do a few months earlier. Still, we did not leave the electric light on during the day because Daddy explained to us that electricity was very expensive. But best of all, that electric light put off a lot more illumination so a person could see much better.

There were only four of us for supper since Frances was at college getting her provisional degree so she could come back to Virgil and teach the following fall. What I didn't know at the time was that she would be my second grade teacher when school started in September.

Daddy looked at me again and noticed, "Robert, you didn't take your dirty clothes off before coming in!" Mamma then said, "Oh Bill, it's okay. I am having such a hard time getting our clothes washed with all this rain anyway. I still have clothes out there in one of the tubs that I couldn't get out to dry today. We really need some sunshine." I could see the stress on my mother's face; all this rain was beginning to wear on everyone.

The supper conversation started with Mamma telling us of getting a letter from Frances. She had written that it was raining in Emporia and there was fear the Cottonwood River would overflow south of town and she might not be able to get home this next weekend. This was sad news. She always came home to get her clothes washed and ironed. Besides, we would just really miss her.

Mamma then asked me, "Robert, you were out in the barn today, what were you up to? Not mischief I hope." I quickly answered, "Oh, no, Mamma. I found four new kittens that were so soft and they just wanted me to cuddle them. They had just opened their eyes. Oh, Mamma, they were so cute, I just had to hold them. They were so soft."

Then Daddy spoke up and said when he went to town today and crossed over the big black bridge, he could see the water was running high and, in some places, it was already out of its banks. It wasn't looking good.

Supper was one of my favorite meals and this one was especially memorable. It consisted of homemade bread which Mamma had made that morning, sliced tomatoes, corn-on-the cob, sliced onions and cucumber salad, fried potatoes with onions (all this from the garden) along with a fried chicken that Mamma butchered that afternoon from the flock she raised especially for eating. They were commonly known as spring chickens—tender and very delicious, rolled in flour, then fried in lard.

I took my favorite pieces of chicken, the gizzard and the legs; Daddy took his share along with his favorite, the liver; and as always, Mamma ate the neck. She knew no one else would eat it if she didn't. It was a family joke that by eating the neck you would become beautiful, but I'm not sure anyone was convinced. As we ate, the dogs waited outside patiently; they knew some good chicken bones were on the way.

Then we had angel food cake, my favorite dessert. I loved it as I did most meals Mamma fixed. She was really a good cook. Anyway, that is what Daddy told everybody.

Mamma asked my father, "Bill, you went to town this afternoon what did they talk about?" He nodded. "I stopped by the Robison garage to get a piece welded for the corn planter and they were talking about whether we would have another big flood this year." She frowned and said, "That's all we need. It is getting late in the season and no time to replant the crops if they get destroyed." Then she went on talking about the flood in '48 and how bad it was.

"Don't you remember the house the Hills lived in that washed away over at the Skelly Pump Station?" Mr. Hill ran the pump station there for Skelly Oil. Marilyn chimed in, "They were that family with all those kids. Their house washed away, losing everything, and they were lucky to get out with their lives." Mamma remarked, "The Lord must have been looking after them."

With the rain continuing, I said to Marilyn, "We will have to go down tomorrow and see if the river is out of its banks." This was something we always did when the water rose. We put a stick in the mud so the next time we checked, we could see if the water was rising or falling.

We sat there as a family talking about the other things that had happened that day, as we did most every day after supper. I guess you would say that was our family hour, a time to visit about everything—family happenings, local gossip or world news, if we had any. This was a time of family bonding, a feel-good time. It usually included lots of laughter.

Marilyn started helping Mamma clear the table and they washed the dishes. Soon Mamma announced, "I'm going to separate the milk." Another chore that had to be done every day and produced a small amount of money for household and personal needs.

The next morning, Marilyn and I headed down the lane to the river bottom. The narrow path, only big enough to get a tractor up and down, was very steep and slick, and had numerous ruts eroded into the path because of all the rain, making it hard to keep our balance. The ground we were walking on was very muddy and a real challenge to keep upright.

The path started just south of our milk barn and went into a canopy of trees, almost like an entrance to a dark cave. The trees stretched their limbs over the lane. As we went forward, there was a constant dripping of water on us from the trees above. It felt like a tropical rainforest without the monkeys, but there were many birds flying around the trees and singing while enjoying the break in the rain.

The barn swallows flew so fast and caught insects as they went along. Those birds could dive and turn so quickly, they seemed to be flying almost at the speed of light. In addition, there were lots of sparrows, and even a covey of quail that took flight and scared us both. Then a beautiful red bird flew directly in front of us. It was just so pretty. Marilyn told me, "That was a cardinal." I hoped we could see more of these. Then there was an old grouchy blue jay, sounding off in his hateful voice, seeming to tell everything around him he was unhappy. He wanted us all to know it.

We even found a box turtle crawling up the hill. Marilyn mentioned, "Those turtles crawl up away from the rising flood water. They know what is going to happen and I don't think they are very good swimmers."

We continued down the hill and started to hear a roar of the running flood water. This roar was not extremely loud but constant, and it felt like it completely surrounded us. This was like nothing I had ever heard before, and it smelled, not as bad as the pigpen, but it sure wasn't pleasant. This smell caused a muddy taste in our mouths.

We could see water starting to snake its way across the field. By afternoon, it started raining and rained all day and all night. The next day we went to check if the water was rising. The water was now totally out of the riverbanks and running across the field, even up to the foot of the hill. Later that day it started to rain again and rained all night again.

When we went to check the next time, the flood water had started to creep up the side of the hill. We put the first stick into the mud to mark where the water line was and then went to tell Daddy what we had seen. He then decided that he needed to go down and check on the Biglers who lived at the foot of the hill by what was called the Hanson ford at the time. He encouraged them to come up and stay at our house, but they declined. Instead, they asked Daddy if he would hook up his tractor to pull their trailer that had a hog in it up the hill. Daddy told them he would just take the hog to our place. And he did. Later we found out that the flood water had gotten into their house and ruined a lot of things. That poor old couple.

The following weekend, Frances was not able to get home from college as feared. The river was out of its banks south of Emporia and blocked Kansas Highway 99 leading south to Madison, and on to Hamilton where the turnoff was east to Virgil.

It kept raining and we kept moving the marker up the hill.

Henry Hanson, who lived farther up the road, drove into our yard. I yelled my customary, "We got company." He pulled up to where my father was standing and looked out his window. "Bill, I just tried to get into town and the river is really up and across the road on the other side of the big bridge." Henry then drove off slowly and mud went everywhere.

Marilyn and I were going down to see where our stick was now and Daddy decided he wanted to go with us this time. The water was really up and it looked like a dark brown ocean, running very dirty. You could see the brown swirling water with white foam being carried in the current, plus large trees which had been uprooted and now floating away. Some had their leaves still attached. One particularly large tree was lying flat in the water with its huge ball of roots leading and looking as if it were a large ship. It was really big and got about halfway across the field when it came to a stop. Daddy said in a disgusted voice, "That big monster will be hard to get out if it is there when the water goes down."

The running floodwater produced an eerie sound along with its constant roar. The sound seemed like it had tremendous power. Then periodically, you could hear the sound of a couple of cawing crows as they flew over all that disgusting brown water. It was not a pretty sight, and when we looked to the east, it seemed like the dirty water would never end. What a river!

Daddy commented, "This is almost beyond belief; this is the highest I have ever seen it. I thought the flood of '48 was bad, but nothing like this." We walked back up the hill with no one saying a word. You could tell from Daddy's voice and facial expressions that this was really bad. He kept taking his hat off and pushing his hair backward in what seemed to be a nervous reaction, and saying in a low voice, "I can't believe it."

The flood finally went down and Daddy remarked, "This flood outdid the one in '48 and I thought that one was bad," echoing what Mamma said earlier. Daddy set a fence post at the high-level mark and said, "I am sure this will never be this high again in my lifetime." He was right. And now seventy-some years later, the water has never gotten close to anything like in the flood of '51.

Crops and cattle were our main source of income and with

no crops, we had nothing to feed the cows or pigs the upcoming winter, or grain to sell. I, years later, wondered what was going through my mother and father's minds as they looked across the flooded Verdigris River Valley. Were they thinking about all the work it had taken to put in those crops or were they thinking about finances and how they were going to be able to make it? Floods had happened on the Verdigris River before, but never this bad. Finances were never discussed with the children and this was no different. But even a six-year-old can sense when something is really wrong. It didn't cross my mind for a number of years, but I wondered if Daddy ever thought he had spent too much money for Mickey.

The National Weather Service site https://www.weather.gov/top/1951_flood stated that:

> The excessive rainfall during May, June, and July 1951 resulted in frequent periods of severe flooding throughout Kansas and adjacent states during late spring and early summer. The flooding actually began in June and continued into mid July. Extremely heavy rains of 8 to 16 inches fell from July 9 - 13 culminating in the highest river stages since the Great Flood of 1844. July 13, 1951, can be rightly designated as the single day of greatest flood destruction in Midwestern United States history to that date. On July 13, the Kansas River crested at all official gaging stations, from Manhattan to Bonner Springs, at 4 to 6 feet above all previous recorded crests. The Marais Des Cygnes, Neosho and Verdigris Rivers were also at or near crests; exceeding all previous records by as much as 9 feet.

I visited with a number of people who lived around the Virgil area during the Flood of 1951 and they shared the following memories:

Margret (Berry) Culp, a fellow classmate of mine, was seven at the time of the flood and a member of the 1962 class. She remembered seeing people playing in the floodwater in the fields just west of Virgil, in close proximity to the railroad depot. She said her mother would not allow her to do that because the water was too dirty. Smart mother.

Gary Bowman, age 11 at the time of the flood and a member of the 1957 graduating class lived south of the Virgil cemetery on what was known as the "old hill road" going to Quincy, about four miles outside of Virgil. He recalled going along with his mother and father to Virgil for some grocery supplies, and they had not been gone more than one hour. Then on the way back to their house, they found flood water across the road north of the cemetery. It was so deep they were unable to cross it. They parked their pickup on high ground and started walking south, staying on the high ground until they reached their house.

Julie (Harris) McKenzie, age 11 at the time of the flood and a member of the 1957 graduating class, lived south of Virgil on the west side of the old river road. The flood was about three feet into their house. Julie said it was up almost to the keyboard of the piano. The other furniture on the first floor had been carried up to the second floor to keep it dry.

The mud and silt were so bad they brought in the scoop shovels to clear the house. Then they brought in the water hose to finish washing the house. They moved into Virgil to live with Julie's grandparents until the house was cleaned and put back together.

Monte Commons, age 10 at the time of the flood and a member of the 1957 graduating class. They lived on Main Street beside their grocery store. The water never made it up that high. Monte said, "As I recall, the floodwater came all the way up past the railroad tracks and got into a few houses that were down in that area of town. I remember going down by the depot to visit my friends in the Hays family. I do not remember if the water got into their home, but I know it was at least close to where they lived. I do remember seeing large carp swimming in the ditches near the depot and people using pitchforks to spear them. I don't remember if there were any gar, but I would suspect there were."

I asked Monte about how his parents worked with flood victims who were their customers. He said the following: "I am sure that my folks had to carry some people on credit for groceries a while longer after the flood and until people got back to work and generated some income." Years later I was told by my oldest sister Freda that my parents were unable to meet all their obligations and had to sell their small herd of beef cattle. The Commons were very understanding and easy to work with. This is where the local grocer not only sold groceries, but also served as the banker. Virgil was fortunate, to not only have a farming community, but also a large number of oil workers who were paid monthly and did not have to wait until harvest for their income.

Keith Dalton, age 10 at the time of the flood was a member of the 1957 graduating class. His family lived north of Virgil on the road to Hilltop and farmed in the Verdigris valley. One of the first things Keith talked about was that in 1951, there were fifty-one inches of rain in fifty-one days, and it rained every day during that time period. He remembered they had to move both hogs and cattle to higher ground to avoid the flood water. In addition, they had to move both a corncrib and some hay to avoid losing them to the flood. The final thing was cleaning the flooded fields of debris after the water receded back into the river banks. Of course, this process could not be started before the ground dried out.

This one disaster definitely made more of an impact on the people of the area than anything else I know of, and for some it took years to overcome their setback. For others, they never recovered completely. There was already a migration of farm families leaving the 160-acre farms, but this only accelerated it.

The rain finally stopped, the flood water went down, the ground dried up, but life never returned to normal; it was just different. No crops to harvest and no hay to put up. It had all been destroyed. All of us, for a period of time, seemed to move around with little enthusiasm, no spring in our step and little happiness shown on our faces. Even the dogs seemed to be a little more forlorn.

The impact of this flood, and the immediate twelve months following, affected our lives for many years to come.

Chapter 25

Greenwood County Fair

It was Saturday, August 22, 1951—a beautiful day which was probably going to get hot before it was over. The sun was just starting to come up over the hills across the Verdigris Valley and Daddy had just finished the milking and was walking back to the house with a milk bucket in his hand. The dogs were jumping around aggravating each other, first running in front of Daddy and then behind him.

Then the rooster started to crow its "cock-a-doodle-do." I heard Daddy come in the back porch and the screen door slammed behind him. I got out of bed and went into the kitchen where Mamma was cooking breakfast. She poured me a cup of coffee and added the cream and sugar. I sat down at the table, still in my Roy Rogers pajamas. Then Daddy sat down at the table and Mamma handed him his coffee.

I could still hear that old rooster crowing. He was just loud and obnoxious. I didn't see how anyone or anything could sleep through that racket. Well, maybe my sisters could. About that time Marilyn came stumbling down the stairs, rubbing her eyes trying to wake up. When Mamma said the customary, "Good morning, sunshine," Marilyn only grunted a reluctant "good morning" in return. Maybe that is all you could expect from a fourteen-year-old.

A few minutes later, Frances followed with a much more cheerful look on her face while saying good morning to everyone. Just then the rooster crowed loudly again. Daddy commented, "That old rooster can quit crowing now that everyone is up," although it didn't stop. He then joked, "Mabel, I know what we can have for dinner on Thanksgiving Day…that old rooster!"

Mamma chuckled and joined the revelry. "Bill, that old rooster would be so tough that I would have to start cooking it today to have it ready by Thanksgiving!"

Mamma had cooked a lot of fried eggs, bacon, and pancakes, enough for a thrashing crew. We all started eating when a few minutes later Daddy commented, "Mabel, I saw a poster for the county fair yesterday while at the Robison Garage. I was thinking of us all going there today. How would that be with you?"

She immediately agreed saying, "Bill, I don't need anything from the store this week so it would be okay for me. In fact, it would be nice to get away. It might be cooler there than around this place."

I chimed in, "Oh, I guess it would be okay if I didn't ride Mickey today." So, we were set. The family was going to the County Fair, even Frances the new teacher. This was bound to be a lot of fun, I thought. But I had to ask, "What about our baths?" hoping Mamma would say we could just skip them this week.

Instead, she said, "We can do that tomorrow." That was okay with me, except it would have been better if we had just skipped this week all together. I didn't like baths.

Everyone changed into their Saturday night clothes and we had a very early dinner before heading out. We got into our car and sat in our designated places, Marilyn and Frances in the backseat and me in between Daddy and Mamma. This wasn't a good place for me because Mamma had a very good view of my ears. I really hoped she wouldn't see any dirt today. I guess I got lucky as I didn't hear her usual admonishment of "Robert, those are the dirtiest ears I have ever seen." Under my breath I said, "Thank you, Lord."

We pulled away from the farm, still not going too fast when Daddy opened the door and spit some of his tobacco out onto the road. Mamma repeated her usual, "Bill, I really wish you would give up that bad habit." My father just sighed. "Maybe tomorrow," and on we went.

Soon we were approaching Hamilton and past the rodeo arena when Frances said, "Look! There is where Freda met Floyd Wayne, and now they are married." Looking at Marilyn, she teased, "Maybe they will have another rodeo someday and you can meet your man." And then she laughed.

Shortly, we drove into Eureka and Daddy pulled into the fairgrounds big parking lot which already had a lot of cars in it. We pulled into a parking spot and slowly got out. Mamma said, "Robert, I don't want you to get lost so stay close to me. Marilyn and Frances, you help watch him for me too."

I had no idea where they thought I was going. I could ride Mickey all over the countryside and not get lost. They probably had forgotten I had passed the first grade. I was responsible for myself. Anyway, I thought so.

There was a lot of music and noise, and somebody on a loudspeaker was announcing different things but I couldn't understand any of it. Then there were lots of rides: a merry-go-round; a Ferris wheel; and some ponies going in a circle, round and round. I told Mamma that I wanted to ride those ponies. She replied very firmly, "Now you have a horse at home that doesn't cost you anything. Why would you want to pay to ride one here just going around and around?" Nothing more was said about ponies. She was right.

Daddy suggested we go look at the animals and off we went into what is called an open-air barn. The first thing we saw were the most beautiful horses, but of course they couldn't compare to Mickey.

Frances started looking at the cards hanging on each stall and, before long, she excitedly hollered out, "This one is owned by Dick Berry and he got a blue ribbon." She reminded us, "I used to babysit for him and his sisters." His sister Jill was in my class and I would be seeing her as soon as school started. I had a crush on her and could hardly wait because I thought she was pretty and smart.

Then on to the pigs we went. There were lots of them—big ones, small ones, and even one with a litter of little pigs. I thought they were so cute. These pigs had all been given a bath and they looked so clean, not like ours that always had mud all over them.

Before long, Frances and Marilyn wandered off somewhere, but Mamma, Daddy and I kept looking at the animals. Next were the cows. Oh, how beautiful they all were, as they too had been given a bath. Their washed tails were so white on the ends and it looked like they had fluffed up the hair on the end to make it look cleaner. This was different from our cows where they had manure caked in the tails and looked kind of brownish. These for sure were not our cows.

My sisters soon came back, but Daddy had seen one of our neighbors and wanted to go talk with him so the rest of us continued to the next barn where they had chickens. There was a black chicken, red chickens and white ones. There were even brightly colored ones with red heads, and some even had green trim with a brown body. Some of the chickens were in a single cage and others were six or more in a larger cage. Mamma kept reading the cards attached and was delighted to share, "Girls look here. These are Ronnie Aeschliman's," and there was a blue ribbon on them. "I knew the Aeschlimans had some good chickens."

Years later I talked with Ronnie and he told me that the whole family would get in the car and go to the fair. It was one of their annual family outings, just like my family. Today he sometimes makes an entry now and then for food and photographs, but not chickens.

Daddy rejoined us and suggested we get a lemonade to drink. I believe it cost about fifty cents for all of us. They were really good, but Daddy still thought that was a lot of money. Mamma just reminded him that "everything costs more here at the fair."

Mamma wanted to go where the baked goods were and we walked to another barn. This one had lots of great looking pies and cakes, along with a lot of cupcakes. All the pies had a piece cut out of them. I was told by Frances that was so the judge could see the inside. Then we started looking at the cupcakes and I wanted to eat one, but Marilyn said, "No, you can't." Frances kept looking at the tags on them and then noticed there were some cupcakes with Judith Kimbell's name on them along with a blue ribbon.

In this barn were lots of fresh vegetables, including many in glass jars. I thought they were so pretty. I saw canned carrots, tomatoes, green beans, corn, and many other things. And they all had ribbons hanging on them.

At the other end of this barn were some things that had been sewed—tea towels, aprons, hot pads, dresses and girls' slips. Frances was looking over these things and excitedly said, "Look here, these two slips are made by Judith Kimbell and Julie Harris. They both have blue ribbons."

I remember Mamma's reaction. "That's great! All the Virgil things we have seen are blue ribbon winners. This speaks highly of our 4H Club and community."

In the 1950s, 4H was a major part of life in rural Kansas. It taught many skills that future homemakers would need, even though many of the skills aren't necessary today. How many people now have a sewing machine or pressure cooker for canning? Then, too, there is no way to raise a hog in your backyard either.

Next, we came across displays created by each 4H Club. They were all different, but one really stood out to me, probably because it had a toy tractor. It was on a large table with a miniature farm on it. Everything was perfect. The fields were green and the crop rows were very straight. This impressed my father who mentioned that "neighbors drive by just to see how straight your rows are." The display also had a farmhouse, barn, chicken house, milk barn and corncrib plus horses, cows for both milk and beef, pigs, chickens, and more. It looked so perfect except they only left one thing out. They didn't have an outhouse. Oh well, only a six-year-old would notice that detail.

I just wanted to crawl up on the table and start playing. To me, this was the best exhibit of the whole fair. It made such an impression on me that I loved it and kept looking at it time and time again.

Before long I overheard my father say, "Mamma, do you think we should be going? Those old cows aren't going to milk themselves." Soon we were heading toward the car and on our way home. I don't think we got any further than out on the road when I fell asleep. This had been a very fun day at the Greenwood County Fair.

Virgil 1952, Second Grade

Second grade was going to be a special year because my new teacher would be my sister Frances. But I also knew this was going to be difficult for me to deal with. First of all, I was told that I couldn't call her Frances; I needed to address her as Miss Phillips. That was a lot to ask of a six-year-old boy. Besides, not calling my sister by her first name, she was not going to be living at home. She was going to be staying with another teacher, Miss Mamie Allis, who taught the third grade. She lived just across the street from the school but Frances planned to come home on the weekends.

Then, of course, there was the issue that if I got in trouble at school, Frances would tell our parents. In the end, I guessed this wouldn't be that different since we had shared the same parents all of our lives and she had already told on me many times. But I knew trouble was just around the corner. I had an intuition about these sorts of things.

What a predicament! My sister who still lived at home was going to ride the school bus with me every day, and then another sister was going to be with me all day at school. I had no way to win. Although I know there were a couple of small advantages, I can't think of them right now, but maybe give me a few days.

The summer seemed to have gone by very fast, and it had been eventful—getting my dream horse, the terrible flood of 51, my Grandma Young dying (the only grandparent I had ever known), and I had outgrown most of my clothes. I didn't think they looked small but my mother had other thoughts about my appearance.

Then the day came, summer was over and school was to start. It was such a wonderful morning with the sun shining, very few clouds, some crows off in the timber going "caw, caw,

caw" and then flying as if they had some place to go but landing only a short distance away. Marilyn and I were waiting outside while calmly petting the dogs. Riding the bus now was no big thing since I had done this all of last year. In fact, I considered myself quite experienced now.

Soon, we heard the rattling of the bus, the dogs barked and we yelled to Mamma that the school bus was coming. In a cloud of dust, the bus roared into our barnyard. I took a good look at it and noticed that the broken window from the previous year was now replaced, and I thought this was progress. It looked like they might have even washed the bus, but it was already fairly dirty by the time it reached our place.

A unique thing about Virgil's bus drivers was that the majority of them were juniors and seniors in high school, which today I find most astonishing. One of those drivers was Dale Sauder who would later become my brother-in-law. He would leave the school with a load of students and, by the time he got to the end of his route, he would be at his home. He left the bus there overnight and, in the morning, drive the route backwards, picking up the students as he returned to school. It amazes me the responsibility that these seventeen-year-olds took on, and that the school administrators had so much trust in them. It was certainly a different era; youngsters just grew up and matured at an earlier age. Case in point, how many kids do you know who can drive a tractor and kill a chicken for dinner, all at the age of five?

As we boarded the bus, Daddy came walking out of the barn and yelled, "Don't give that new teacher too much trouble." I knew he was proud of my sister and so was Mamma. Three of her daughters had now followed in her footsteps to become teachers.

I got on the bus and sat down next to Raymond Engle. Since we lived relatively close to each other, we had spent a lot of time together that summer. I was now six years old and allowed to wander a little more around the countryside, plus I had a horse to ride and could get back and forth a lot faster. All of that made it easier to visit my friends.

Finally, the dust encircled the bus like a cyclone and we were on our way to another year at Virgil Grade School. The noise level of everyone trying to talk over each other became really loud, but in a short period of time, we were at that old black bridge. It shook, rattled, swayed, squeaked and then finally we were across it, just like in the past. In a few more minutes the bus pulled up in front of the school and, when the driver took hold of the door handle to open the door, out we went.

The moment of truth would soon be upon me. Was I going to be treated as special or was I going to be just another second grader? I thought I had a good chance of becoming the teacher's pet, although this honor had gone to one of the girls in our class last year and most likely would be a girl again. But, still, I was the teacher's little brother.

I looked toward the school but didn't see anything of Miss Phillips. She hadn't come out to meet me, "the special one." Lots of things rushed through my mind. How was it going to be having a teacher I had tied to a chair and roped, and who lots of times played tricks on me? We had a lot of history together. She was the best tractor driver in the hayfield, she had taken me fishing, and once in a while even let me have her chewing gum off the headboard of the bed.

Raymond and I turned to go into our classroom and there she was. Frances looked very busy and simply told me that my desk was over there by the window. With no hug or special hello, I soon knew I was just another student as far as she was concerned. What a letdown!

I decided to start saying hello to my other classmates: Myrna Pennebaker, the first girl I had ever kissed, and Jill Barry who I had started liking the previous year. This was after Miss Lewis had talked to me and Myrna about showing our affection too openly, and driven a dagger through my heart. Now being an upperclassman, those girls just looked so much prettier.

We had a new group of students who were the first graders now: Audrey Shaw, Mary Lou Fisher, Robert Johnson and a bunch more. Since I was an upperclassman, I knew my way around the school and playground. This playground consisted of swings, merry–go-round, teeter-totters and a very high slide. This equipment was also of the industrial type and the frames of each piece were made of very solid iron pipe. The swing would let you go, I think, as high as thirty feet in the air. The slide was also very high, maybe twenty-five feet and it took a long time to climb to the top of the ladder. Finally, the bell rang and the year officially started.

The first thing we did was say the Lord's Prayer and the Pledge of Allegiance to the flag. Then we sat down. I was so lucky because I was sitting directly behind Jill Berry. Maybe this might present an opportunity to whisper back and forth. Just being close was a good thing I thought, but soon learned Miss Phillips had other ideas.

At last, the dismissal bell rang and the first day of school was over. I had avoided all day having to call my sister "Miss Phillips." But here she was coming up to me as I walked to the bus. She said, "Robert, tell Mamma I will be home this week-end." I confirmed, "I sure will," still never once calling her Miss Phillips. Then I got on the bus for the ride home.

I actually thought it was going to be wonderful having my sister home again. Even though Frances and I now had this strange relationship, I loved her a whole lot. I could hardly wait to tell Mamma that Miss Phillips was going to be home this weekend! The bus stopped, the driver opened the door, and the dogs were waiting for us as usual, but I had no time to stop and pet them. I had to find Mamma to tell her the good news. I ran all the way from the bus into the house and yelled, "The teacher is coming home for the weekend." I think Mamma was as excited as I was.

Finally, it was Friday and school was out for the weekend. I got on the bus and sat down beside Raymond Engle. We bounced down the rough road to the old black bridge where we had to wait for another car to cross that was coming from the other direction. Then it was our turn to again drive over the bridge, bumping, shaking, and rattling while it squeaked, swayed and even moaned a little before we were over it safely.

This time, there was a dead skunk in the middle of the road and it smelled really bad. The smell was so bad that everyone on the bus yelled "phew" at the same time while holding our noses. I even remember my eyes burning from the smell. I also think the driver hit the dead skunk with one of the bus's front tires on purpose, which only made it worse. High school drivers may have been mature enough to drive a bus load of students, but they still were immature when it came to some of their actions, like hitting a skunk (dead or alive), if given a chance.

We traveled on down the road and finally dropped off all the other students before reaching our home. The bus still smelled of skunk, and even the dogs wouldn't come very close to it.

As usual, we completed our chores—the cows were milked and the other chores finished, and we headed to the house for supper. After eating, we talked about how the first week of school went until Marilyn got up to get ready for a date with Dale Sauder.

Finally, it was my bedtime and I was tired and wanted to get to sleep fast. Frances was expected home later that night and I wanted to get up early to see her in the morning, and maybe we could do something fun. For a while, I lay in bed listening to the coyotes yip and howl. They scared me a little but I finally went to sleep.

The next morning, while it was still dark outside, I heard my mother in the kitchen. I rolled out of bed and immediately went to where she was and asked her, "Did the teacher come home last night?" I was happy and excited when Mamma said, "She sure did." Then without saying another word, I headed up the stairs in a dead run to wake Frances up. I could hear my mother say, "Let her sleep," but by that time I was jumping right in the middle of her bed.

In the second grade I started realizing that I had a big problem with reading. I knew I was looking at the words but they weren't registering in my brain. It wasn't because of bad eyesight; it was just comprehension. This learning disability has followed me my entire life. I didn't talk with anyone about it for a number of years, even after needing to repeat the fifth grade, and finally being assigned to a special reading class. I had no idea at the time what my problem was. Sometimes in class we didn't have enough books for everyone so we had to sit side-by-side and read the same book. I was reading so slowly that the person sitting beside me would become impatient and want me to hurry up. Not to be embarrassed, I would simply not read and then turn the page when my reading-mate was done.

Eventually, the ultimate measure of my reading skills was

tested. We each had to read a book and give a report on it. We were to choose a book from our classroom library, read it, and then stand up in front of the class to report what we had read. The book I chose was about a pair of bald eagles and their babies. The book was in full color and the pages showed how the mother and father eagle went about choosing a site for the nest, and then the mother laying two eggs. The story went on to tell how the baby eagles were cared for and how they grew and finally left the nest. As I look back, maybe this story was a comparison to our lives as we were growing up and would soon leave our parents. But at the time, someday leaving home never crossed my mind.

It finally came time for my report. I stood up and told the story and got a great review from Miss Phillips. But I knew in my heart that I hadn't read the book at all. I had simply looked at the beautiful pictures, and there were a lot. I even wondered what would happen when there were no pictures in a book. I knew I would be in trouble, and as a matter of fact, this trouble followed me through life as I mentioned earlier. I found ways to partially overcome this disability, but it took years, plus taking a toll on my confidence.

I could sense that things weren't as happy around our farm, but couldn't figure out what it was. Looking back through time, I questioned if it was the stress brought on by the great flood of 1951. After all, we didn't have any corn to pick and only got one hay crop in that year. It also seemed that Mamma was tired a lot, but she still did all her summer work, like planting the garden and all that canning.

Chapter 27 ℞

Cattle Drive

It was in mid-September 1951 that for a short time I became a real cowboy. The morning was superb. The Flint Hills were still somewhat green from a summer that had seen a record rain fall. We were going to drive our beef cattle to the Virgil rail head that day. It was just like those cowboys who had been doing it since the 1870s, driving their cattle to Abilene or maybe Dodge City. Maybe it would be like Roy Rogers rounding up his cattle on the RR Bar Ranch. I was six years old but would become seven in just a couple of months—still a young boy who could conjure up a million different ideas in his head.

I rolled out of bed knowing we were going to have a very busy day. I went into the kitchen where Mamma was fixing breakfast. She had already been out to milk the cows while Daddy had done the rest of the chores. Mamma poured a cup of coffee for me and a cup of milk in my Roy Roger's cup. She then put a big platter of fried eggs, along with bacon and pancakes, on the table. Soon, Daddy came inside and sat down and said, "Son, you better eat up. We have a big day ahead of us." Oh, how good that made me feel! I was going to be part of the work group and do it on my horse. I thought I had lived my whole life just for this day.

Shortly after, Marilyn stumbled down the steep stairs and asked why we were up so early. I told her we were driving the cattle to the stockyards today. I asked her, when she got to school, to remind my sister and teacher, Miss Phillips, that I was going to be gone for the next couple of days. I knew my mother had talked with Frances previously, but just wanted to make sure she wouldn't forget and wonder where I was. Then for good measure, I added, "Marilyn, you will have to ride the bus today by yourself." I felt so grown up and somewhat important.

About a week before, Daddy and I had gone to the Virgil train depot to order a cattle car to be brought in for us to use. Mr. Johnson was the station superintendent and took the order. In the background I could hear the constant clicking of the telegraph.

Mr. Johnson went over to the window where the telegraph was clicking away and tapped his finger for a little while. He then came back to where we were standing and handed my father a piece of paper saying he would see Daddy next week. And then he turned to me. "Robert, are you going to help drive those cows?" I remember my excited reply well. "Yes, sir! I will be there helping."

Mr. Johnson's son Robert was in the first grade, just a year behind me. We were in the same room and we both had my sister Miss Phillips as our teacher. Virgil, being a small town, was where almost everybody knew everyone else. That was pretty nice unless you were doing something improper (something you would get into trouble doing) and someone told your parents or, in some cases, your sister.

On the way home after getting the cattle car ordered, I asked my father, "We aren't going to sell Heifer, are we?" My father hesitated and reluctantly answered, "Son, I am sorry but we need to."

Tears started running down my cheeks but I was a cowboy and big boys and cowboys don't cry. That was the last anything was said about selling Heifer.

The next morning after breakfast was over, Daddy and I headed for the barn. About that time the old rooster gave out a big "cock-a-doodle-do." Daddy said, "I think that old boy is a little late again. Maybe it's time to get a new one who doesn't sleep so late." Then the dogs came running up and jumped all over me, but I wasn't going to school, so I guessed that was okay.

Daddy had already gathered his horse and Mickey before breakfast, giving both of them a scoop of oats so they were ready to brush down. We only had one problem—we had one bridle and one saddle. Since Daddy's horse was not very well broken in and Mickey was just wonderful, Daddy got both the bridle and saddle. It was okay since I had been riding Mickey most of the time without a saddle anyway. Instead, Daddy gave me a halter with a lead rope and told me I could handle her just like those Indian braves did their horses while hunting buffalo. Besides, I just couldn't see Daddy riding bareback.

We were ready to ride when Henry Hanson rode up on his horse and joined us. Daddy had talked to him earlier about helping. Daddy gave me a lift up onto Mickey and we were ready to ride for the brand WP (William Phillips). We started down the gravel road and headed to the pasture where the cows were located. Mickey and I had gone this way many, many times to visit Raymond Engle who lived just down the road.

It was such a nice day with a light breeze blowing into our faces, sun shining bright, birds flying all around, and with only one or two fluffy clouds in the sky. A lone hawk was soaring very high in the sky and about a dozen crows flew over by the timber calling "caw, caw, caw."

This was also the way we went to get the mail each day, which sometimes just Mickey and I would do. Everything was going fine when we reached the corner to where Mickey and I would always turn to go to the Engle's place. I forgot this was where I always turned Mickey and headed her at a dead run the rest of the way to Raymond's.

The next thing I knew, Mickey was running as fast as she could toward my friend's place. Without a bridle and no bit, there was no stopping her. My father, who was a very good rider, quickly moved to save the day. He turned his horse after us, but we had already surged ahead by approximately ten yards. Kicking his horse in the sides, he soon over-took us and grabbed the lead rope on my horse to pull her to a stop. By this time, my heart was beating fairly fast. I guess Mickey thought since we were at this place, it was time to turn and run.

After the excitement, we then continued on, passing by the Hawkins' home, to the intersection where the road goes across the old black bridge and in to Virgil. This is where we turned westward. This was also the first time I realized we were going to drive the cows over that bridge. I wasn't sure how Mickey or the cows were going to handle this. I knew the bridge was going to squeak, shake, moan and sway. I thought since Daddy must know everything about horses and cows, it would be okay.

The three of us turned westward and rode about a half mile where we came to a pasture gate on the north side of the road. Daddy got off his horse and opened it for us and we rode through. Daddy then closed the gate and we started the round up. This pasture was owned by the Hawkins and we just rented it.

There were no cows in sight, so this meant they all must be in the timber or over the hill. We rode north and after entering the trees, we saw some of the cows. It was then I came upon the most beautiful small waterfall. I had never seen anything like this before. What a charming setting! I sat there for a moment or two, just admiring what I was seeing and taking in all the beauty. For years I really wondered if I had really seen such a sight or if it was just part of a little boy's imagination. My answer came seventy-two years later while visiting with Janice (Hawkins) Casey, the daughter of Floyd. I asked her if such a place really did exist on their farm. She said that it did and, to her knowledge, this spring had never run dry.

It was now time to get back to driving cattle and stop admiring the scenery. We worked our way around the woods while driving the cattle out into the open spaces so we could head them toward the pasture gate we had entered through. Daddy got a good count to make sure they were all there.

Daddy rode to the gate and opened it up. He then had me wait at the road and told me not to let any of the cows go west as Henry and he would drive the cattle to the road where I was positioned. Finally, they came and we were on our way headed toward Virgil. I guessed I had done a good job because none of the cows got past me and they all turned east.

After we were on the road, Daddy rode to the front of the cattle and led them through the intersection toward the big black bridge, and then on to the stockyards at Virgil. Henry and I were instructed to get close behind the herd as they approached the bridge and push hard on them.

Daddy's horse gave him a little trouble about going onto the bridge, but soon they were advancing. Next, it was the cows' turn to cross over the bridge. Instead of proceeding, they stopped and Henry and I began yelling, "Get along, get along." After the first one stepped onto the bridge, it was easy from then on. When Mickey and I got to there, I don't think Mickey even was aware and went right on.

Arriving at the stockyards, Daddy already had the gate open to our designated corral and the cows went right in. The cattle car was quickly pulled to the loading chute, and we officially became "cow pokes" by loading the cows. The train would be pulling out in just a couple of hours and the plan was then to drive to the Kansas City, MO Stockyards the next day to meet up with the cows.

(The difference between a cowpoke and a cowboy is, at train loading time, the cowboy would give up his horse for a long stick and then poke the cows, making them get on the train.)

We got up early, before daylight. Mamma had fixed breakfast for us and she told my father she would milk the cows so we could get on the road. After about three hours we arrived at the stockyards. I had never seen so many cattle pens and cattle; it was massive. The stockyards had just re-opened after the big flood of 1951 where over 5,000 head of cattle had drowned. It was deemed to be quite a disaster.

Once there, Daddy talked to a couple of men on horseback, asking where we could find the pens with our cattle, and they told him where to look. Daddy wanted to get another count to make sure they all had arrived and in good shape, so off we went. Once we got to where our cows were, Heifer was in a pen by herself. Daddy asked a man close by why she was separated from the others. He was told that she was really mean and was goring the other cows with her horns. I didn't ask anyone but just crawled over the corral boards, got into the pen, and proceeded to give her a big hug. The man standing there yelled in a very loud voice that it wasn't safe for that little boy to be in there. "He's going get hurt!" My father calmly and proudly replied, "It's okay; he can handle the heifer." I gave her a kiss on the neck and crawled out of the pen. Crawling up the corral to the top board, which was lying flat, there was a deposit of silt about 6 inches high, left there by the '51 flood. I got quite dirty but brushed myself off and was ready to go.

After waiting to get the check for our cows, we got a hamburger at the stockyards and headed back home. I loved hamburgers and it was a real treat to eat one with a bun. At home we didn't eat any with a soft bun. We only had slices of home-made bread that fell apart.

Now I could boast that I had driven cattle to the railhead, taking them from the wonderful Flint Hills grass, helping load them onto the train, and then going to one of the biggest beef markets in the world. This truly was a very big learning experience. I was really hoping that Miss Phillips would look at it that way instead of just a couple of days having fun with my father. But quite honestly, the latter would have been okay too.

Tomorrow I would be back at school, writing my letters again and again. I was starting to understand why my father had dropped out of school after the third grade, especially if he could be around horses every day.

Chapter 28

R♭

Riding My Horse

I woke up with great anticipation of having a wonderful day. It was Saturday so no school. I was in the second-grade and weekends had become very special since I could spend time with my horse, riding anywhere and everywhere. There just didn't seem to be anything better in life than being on the back of Mickey, riding through the valleys and plains of the Kansas Flint Hills and getting lost in the magic of hearing the meadow larks sing and the quail go "bob, bob-white." Off in the distance, seeing a herd of cattle lazily grazing over the hills, this had to be a cowboy's life.

Just as I got out of bed, which was in the living room, Mamma came in from milking the cows and fixed my mostly cream and sugar cup of coffee. In addition, she made a bowl of Post Toasties for me, the cereal of Roy Rogers. I knew this must be good for me because Roy and Dale Evans' pictures were on the cereal box. A year earlier I had gotten enough box tops to send to Post Cereal Company along with a dime to receive a Roy Rogers milk cup, a prized treasure I still have to this day.

I asked Mamma, "Did Daddy leave Mickey in the cow pen?" To my delight, she replied, "Yes, he thought you might want to go riding." I should have asked him the night before to leave her there, but that was a lot to expect of a six-year-old boy to think a whole day ahead when I could hardly think about the next meal. It was nice when your parents thought for you.

After finishing my breakfast, I headed toward the backdoor and I said to my mother, "I'm going out and ride Mickey." As usual, she reminded me, "Wear your coat because it is a little cool out there and be back by dinner time." (This meant noon as we ate supper in the evening.)

I put my coat on, and then went out through the porch and screen door, running toward the barn. I was sure this was almost like Heaven. When the screen door slammed behind me, our three dogs (Happy, Tubsey and Old Shep), who had been lying up against the house enjoying sunning themselves, jumped up and started following. My sisters told me Shep was there when they moved into the house in March of 1944 before I was born. I understand it was somewhat of a custom for tenant farmers to leave their old dog for the next family.

On that fall day in 1951, the sun was shining bright without a cloud in the sky, and a light breeze was blowing which made it a little cool but still very pleasant. The leaves on the trees were falling and about half of them were completely bare. It was a perfect fall day.

I looked toward the milk barn and there, in the pigpen, stood the most beautiful horse ever with a shiny white, brown and black coat. As soon as Mickey saw me, she responded with a neigh and pointed her ears upward. My heart beat a little faster and I ran even quicker toward the big barn to get the bridle. I wondered how could I have been so lucky— loving parents, a horse, three dogs and yes, sisters.

She was my horse and I had waited a number of years for this wonderful experience, and now I was a real cowboy who no longer had to pretend riding with just a stick. After putting Mickey's bridle on, I led her to the barn where I brushed her down. Daddy always insisted that the horses had to be brushed each day they were going to be used. Now it was time to mount. This was the difficult part, because without a saddle, I couldn't pull myself up or jump high enough to get on. But, in the barnyard, it was easy as there was always a hay wagon to lead Mickey alongside, and then crawl up on the wagon to get on. Mickey, although a pretty smart horse, would sometimes step away just as I would be ready to jump on her back. But no matter, I would always make it even if I had to reposition Mickey by the wagon a number of times. I guess I was more determined than she was. Or maybe she just got tired of moving and let me win.

Now I was on top of my horse and on top of the world. It was also time to figure out where I was going. The choices were endless. When I went riding by myself, it took a great deal of planning. I had to consider what gates I was going to go through, plan how I would get back on if I got off, and decide whether to use the saddle which was too heavy to do myself.

I decided on a ride to see Mary Bigler and her brother Bill. Mary was an older lady who always made me feel welcome and usually had something sweet to eat. I don't know how old Mary and Bill were, but to a six-year-old they looked very old. They were of small stature and both had gray hair. They immigrated from Switzerland and spoke with broken English and an interesting accent. They didn't have a car but somehow made it around, maybe a relative who lived in the area. I wasn't sure. They also didn't have a telephone but they were always at home when Mickey and I went to see them.

Every time, Mary seemed very glad to see me. She always wanted me to draw a picture for her that she would put on her wall and I usually drew a horse. I really didn't think there was a nicer person anywhere, except my mother. Mary was nicer than my sisters I knew for sure, even though they were still special to me. But Mary never played tricks on me like my sisters did, and she was always happy to have me around. I can't say the same for my sisters.

The Biglers also had a good place for me to get back on Mickey. So, I was off to see Mary and Bill. The route there was an old road we only used to get to the fields below the hill and down by the Verdigris River. The road was steep with lots of ruts and timber on each side that hung over the road and blocked out most of the sun. It was kind of eerie with lots of different sounds—squirrels, mice, rabbits, possums, raccoons and any number of other four-legged creatures, not to mention the snakes and birds. I felt perfectly safe on my horse and she gave me great confidence that made me brave. I just knew we could outrun everything. This was the same road that Marilyn and I had taken earlier to see what the status of the flood water was.

As I rode along, I could see the effects of the flood. Of course, the short cornstalks were dead and black, and now a few weeds had started to grow again. Then there were lots of driftwood from the flood strewn all over the field, even though Daddy had started to clean it up. The big tree Marilyn and I had seen float over the field was still there.

It wasn't long before I came out of the woods and into the

open field. I turned left heading north, and a short distance ahead I could see Mary and Bill's house. I saw smoke coming from the chimney so I assumed Mary must be cooking or baking something since they cooked with an old, wood-burning cook stove, and it was warm enough that we didn't need the old potbelly stoves for heat. Maybe she thought I would be coming and she was baking some cookies! That had happened a couple of times when I had gone to see them, and Mary knew I really liked oatmeal raisin cookies the best.

Then I thought back to all the times I had come to see Mary. That had been a lot more lately since I had gotten my wonderful horse earlier this spring. Before that, I had to walk and it was well over a mile, a long way for me.

When I first got Mickey and wanted to show her off to Mary, Mamma said, "You can go but you will need to have Marilyn go with you." So, my sister and I rode to their place and I trotted the horse all the way. Marilyn hated the bouncing up and down so much she walked back home after our visit and refused to ride with me ever again. There is more than one way to get rid of a pesky sister! I did love her very much but everything looks different to a six-year-old boy. Sisters were just in the way unless you needed something, such as someone to go with you because your parents wouldn't let you go alone, like fishing in the creek. As I look back, I don't know why I wasn't more understanding of my sisters. They really were very good to me; some things you have you don't know how great they are until they are gone.

Right after I got Mickey, my parents were very protective and wouldn't let me go many places alone, but soon they eased up and I was off to almost anywhere I wanted to go. I just had to be home when they said or my free-roaming would come to a stop. Maybe this would have been something like being grounded.

Now, on this beautiful fall day, I finally arrived at the Bigler place and Mary saw me ride up. She came outside and yelled to me, "Robert, I am glad you came. Tie up your horse and come in." She also asked if Marilyn came with me. I said, "No, I think she was waiting on some boy to come by. I think his name was Dale Sauder. I see them talking a lot at school. I guess they are good friends." (Just about a year after that they were married and had a baby who they named Sheila, and then later a son they named Ronald. They remained married for close to sixty-five years.)

I tied up Mickey and went inside the house. Oh, how warm it felt besides smelling just wonderful! Not being bashful at all I said, "Do I smell some cookies?" Mary quickly answered with a smile. "Would you like to try one? I just baked them." Excitedly with my mouth watering I answered, "Sure."

Mary gave me a cookie and we sat down to visit. I told her all about school, my horse, taking our cows to Kansas City on the train to sell, and many more things. Then I said, "Do you think I could have another one of those cookies?" She said, "Yes, but I don't want you to ruin your appetite for dinner." That made me think. "Oh, is it about dinner time? I better get going, but I will take one of those cookies with me." Running out of the house with cookie in hand, I ran to Mickey, untied her and struggled getting on with my cookie in hand. Finally, I made it on with only losing about half of the cookie. I rode out of their yard and kicked Mickey in the sides, galloping off since we had to hurry along.

I had to get home for dinner so I could spend the rest of the day riding. Being late would not be acceptable. What would be worse is if Mamma made me take a nap. What a waste of time! That summer before school started, I did have to nap every day because of this thing they called polio.

I arrived back home and tied Mickey up at the barn. Then I ran as fast as I could to the house. The dogs came out to greet me, getting in my way every time they could. I ran in the house and Mamma said, "Where is your coat?"

Oh, how could I have forgotten it?! I sheepishly said, "I left it at Mary's." Then Mamma told me I would have to go and get it after dinner. I thought I got a little cold coming home but I was in such a hurry to get home, I didn't think much more about it. This wasn't the first time I had forgotten my coat. It was easy to forget after school. I guess it was just a little boy thing.

Mamma had fixed a cold pickled tongue sandwich for me. We had just butchered a cow and the tongue was very special. She also prepared for me a couple of potato patties using left-over mashed potatoes from the day before. As usual, I had all the milk I wanted to drink. I was kind of picking at my food when Mamma asked, "Did Mary have some cookies for you?"

"Yes, Mamma," I said.

"That Mary is going to spoil you. What did you talk about?"

"We talked about Mickey, the flood last summer, school and riding on the bus, and how good her cookies were."

I finished my dinner and got up from the table telling my mother I was going after my coat. Mamma said, "You get your coat and come back here before you go riding off again. I just want to know where you are and what part of Greenwood County you are going to next."

"Yes, Mamma, I will."

I turned and started to run toward the barn, with the three dogs following. This time, I was running in a gallop like I was on a stick horse. As I got there, I uttered to myself, "Whoa. Whoa up." I guess I had riding horses so much on my mind, that even when I wasn't riding, I pretending to be. I spoke to Mickey telling her, "I didn't water you when we got back, so I must do it now." I led her to the stock tank for a drink and then to the hay wagon for mounting. Then I was off with a "Hi Ho, Silver." I took my time going to Mary's place to get my coat. When I arrived, she said, "I thought you might be back for this. Do you want another cookie?" Of course I couldn't refuse, but remembering how I lost half of my last cookie I replied, "Sure, but could you please hand it to me when I am on Mickey?" She did, and as I was taking the cookie, I thanked her and said, "Hi Ho, Mickey!" Then at a slow trot I rode off toward home again.

This had worked out pretty well; I got three cookies in one day. Quickly, my mind went to wondering where I might go after checking in with Mamma. I thought maybe about riding down by the old Indian grave or to see if Raymond Ingle was home. I got back and checked in with Mamma to tell her I was going to see Raymond, and offered to get the mail from the mailbox. She asked, "How are you going to get back on Mickey if you check the mail?" I told her that I thought I could stay on and lean over far enough to open the mailbox. Satisfied with my answer, Mamma said, "I will see you later and tell Mrs. Ingle I said "Hello."

Riding away, I decided to swing by the old Indian grave on my way to the Ingles' place. The old grave was really just a mound of dirt at the end of our barnyard where the drive turned in. It was about two to three-feet tall and four-feet wide plus ten-feet long. Years before, my sisters made up a tale about the "grave" to scare me, and by now, I knew to question some of their stories. But it sure looked like it could be a grave. I didn't know much about Indians and, since there were none here now, I thought most likely Indians had never been here before. But much to my surprise in doing research of the area, hundreds of native Americans had camped on the farm ground we were using. They were mostly from the Sac and Fox tribes and had camped there during the fall and spring for a number of years. Had I looked closely, arrowheads could have probably been found.

Looking at the mound of dirt and talking previously with my mother, I came to the conclusion that the mound was just an area where someone had built a hothouse for starting garden plants, and it was most likely my family. Sisters can turn a pile of dirt into an Indian grave to add excitement to a little brother's life, or maybe my father had told them this story and they just passed it on.

I rode on south to the Ingles and, not finding anyone home, I decided to go back by the mailbox to see if we had any mail. As I approached it, I looked carefully at how I could get close enough to open the door without getting off Mickey. It seemed possible; I just had to get her close enough and that was the real challenge. Time and time again, I tried and, at last, got close enough to open it. I saw a letter inside but I wasn't close enough to reach in and retrieve it. So now the question was: How could I get back on after I got off to get the letter?

Looking around, I saw a corner post with a brace extending to another post. Holding Mickey's reins and putting the letter inside my coat, I was able to use the barbwires as steps, and then stand on the cross brace while coaxing Mickey close enough to make a jump for her back. I almost landed a little short but was able to pull myself up on her back. I thought, Whew that was close!

I took the letter home and gave it to Mamma. It was from my

Aunt Neva who wrote about herself and Uncle Louis going to see Aunt Gertrude and Uncle Floyd in Colorado. Mamma was always happy to hear from her family.

"Do you want a peanut butter sandwich before you go riding again?" Mamma offered. Eating was always great and I hadn't told her about Mary giving me another cookie, so I readily accepted.

"Sure! Can you put some jelly on it? And could you wrap it up and put it in a bag also?" I thought this was kind of like Mickey and me going on a camping trip. Leaving, I told Mamma, "I am going up toward the Christlieb place and I will be back by supper."

The days were getting shorter and it was easier to know what time it was toward the end of the day. It just got dark earlier. I rode about a mile up by the Christlieb place and saw no one at home. Their dogs came to bark at me so I just kept riding. The Christlieb house was very unique; it stood on some kind of blocks so you could see under it.

Next, I rode a little further and came to the place where my family and I picked gooseberries last summer. This had been as far as I had ever gone so I decided to turn around. I noticed that Daddy had left the pasture gate open so I decided to ride back and explore around. Exploring was a whole lot of fun and, on horseback, it was even more so.

After riding across the pond dam, which was an adventure in itself, I decided to head for a small grove of trees to see what exciting things might be there. After that, I went toward the north fence line and rode beside it for a while, but not finding any places the fence was down, I decided it was time to find a good place to get off Mickey and eat my cowboy sandwich. I found the perfect place.

There was an eroded bank that was just what I wanted. It was the perfect height so I could get up on it and mount Mickey when the time came. Besides that, I could get down off the cutaway and be out of the wind which was good since I had been getting a little chilled. Once I was down in a wonderfully sunny spot, I opened my sandwich. With the sun still shining down and after tying Mickey to a nearby bush, I was able to start eating that delicious treat. I could taste Mamma's love in it.

Oh, how good the warm sun felt! It felt so good I just lay back, and before long was asleep. I think I had a dream that had a coyote in it. I woke up very fast, not sure how long my nap had been, but I thought it best to start home. Picking up my sandwich sack and untying Mickey, I finally got on after a couple of tries and started home.

A small number of clouds had moved in overhead, and the temperature had dropped a few degrees and the breeze increased a little. Oh, what a day it was, but now it was time to ride the trail back home. I started singing a few words of "Back in the Saddle Again" even though I didn't have a saddle. One with saddle bags would have been wonderful because I would have had a place to put my sandwich and I could have hung a canteen of water off the saddle horn.

Riding toward our house I saw a rabbit jump up and run for its life. Momentarily I thought about taking off after it but it disappeared in a flash. As I arrived back home, Mamma and Daddy were just getting ready to start milking the cows. I rode up to them and Daddy jokingly asked if I found any strays out there.

This had been close to the perfect day. Maybe it would have been better if I had had a sidekick to ride along with me. Mickey was a good friend but she never answered back when I asked her questions. But then again, she never did give me bad advice.

Chapter 29

My First Halloween Party

The Halloween party that won't ever be forgotten was October 27, 1951, the Saturday night before Halloween. There was a light breeze blowing which created a feel of fall in the air, and a dimly glowing crescent moon hanging in the sky. There were also a few thin clouds drifting leisurely by, blocking the moonlight now and then.

A small group of us had been invited to a Halloween party and we were starting to arrive at the Kimbell home on Main Street in Virgil. I was six-years-old, somewhat timid, and did not know who was going to be there. This was the first party I had ever been invited to and I felt somewhat uneasy and not sure of what to expect. In other words...I was scared.

My mother had me wear my best school clothes. We didn't dress up in Halloween costumes like kids do today. We just didn't have the money or time to make them.

My sister Frances, who was also my second-grade teacher, took me to the party. She let me out of the car in front of the Kimbell house. As I got out, I could hear the sound of what I thought was two cats fighting. A chill went up my back and I wasn't sure this was going to be fun at all.

I started walking up to the house and I could see a number of eyes looking at me as I cautiously neared the front porch. It was decorated with spider webs and a spider which I couldn't tell was real or not. Regardless, it looked real enough to convince me!

Once on the porch I noticed there were even some big kids there, like in the fifth or sixth grade. Then I saw a friendly face; it was Margaret Berry. She was in my second-grade class at school so I felt somewhat relieved, but still, everything put a great deal of pressure on me not to act afraid. No boy would have wanted to show fear around a girl, and especially a girl in my class.

We finally all went inside the house where the electric lights were on. These lights provided some comfort. Lights were still a big thing for me since my family had just gotten electricity to our farm the year prior. Darkness was a real fear of mine and I carried it with me for a number of years. It might be better said that I was scared of the dark for a large part of my young life.

I noticed right away that there were all kinds of colorful candy, cupcakes and punch on a large table in what must have been their dining room. We didn't have one of these rooms at home since we just ate in the kitchen.

I tried really hard not to be rude and mind my manners as my mother told me when I left home. Everything looked so delicious and I was sure she would think I ate too much. But most importantly, Mamma said, "Now don't you forget to tell Mrs. Kimbell thank you for inviting you to the party."

Suddenly the lights blinked and we all gasped and a few screams were heard. Someone said, "It's time for us all to go out on the porch and hear some stories." We went out to where a number of chairs had been set up in a circle, and we each found one and sat down. It was still dark because, even though they had a porch light, they hadn't turned it on. I thought it was a waste of a good light.

An adult, Mrs. Kimbell I think, stood up and started to talk in a low voice. "I don't know if you all heard about the accident at the old iron bridge just west of town. You know, that old black thing which rattles every time you go over it and feels like you are going to fall through."

Then in a deeper voice the lady said, "Then it happened. A man was coming across so fast that he lost control of his car. It slid sideways, turning over one way and then another before coming to a stop with a big SPLASH in the water, landing on its top. There were body parts scattered all over the place."

"The sheriff asked us to go out and help pick up as much of the remains as we could. So, we did. Now we need your help. You can see or rather feel in this basket; we have a number of parts that we will pass around for each of you to examine." Someone asked, "Do we have to touch them?" The lady said,

"Oh, yes! They won't hurt you because the person is dead and the spirits should have left the body by now." Even though it was dark, everyone's eyes got bigger, even the older kids. Under my breath I said to myself, "You got to be kidding me."

The first thing they passed around was an eye ball, (probably a peeled grape or olive). It was wet, soft and smooth. I was convinced this was crazy. Next was a large bone with pieces of flesh still attached. It looked like a leg. I am sure now that it was a large cow bone, but at the time, I wasn't feeling really good about any of this. It really never came up as to how we were to identify the person. We were all just scared to death about handling the body parts of some stranger. I don't remember any other stories told to us that evening, but maybe I was just in a state of shock so that my ears and mind had shut down.

The party finally ended and it was time to go home. My sister came to pick me up, and since she was a friend of the Kimbells, she came into the house for a short visit. It was probably to see if I had behaved myself. As we were leaving, she wanted to know whether I had told Mrs. Kimbell thank you. I hadn't because I had much more on my mind. Once I located her, I made my way to where she was. In a sheepish voice I said, "Thank you for letting me come to the party. It was wonderful." Mrs. Kimbell smiled and replied, "You are very welcome. It was a pleasure to have you join us."

We didn't have much, but our parents wanted us to be seen as polite and clean in public. I can still remember those spit baths my mother gave me on the way to church with her handkerchief and a little moisture from her mouth. I swear...she could poke her finger into my ear and reach all the way through to the other side. But I was clean.

The party had been fun but I had been scared and I was glad to get out of there. We got into the car and headed home. As we left Virgil, we had to cross the river bridge where the man was killed in the story. I closed my eyes and refused to open them until we were well over the bridge. It did shake and rattle just as the lady telling the story said it did.

What I found very interesting was, while doing research for this book and visiting with Margaret (Berry) Culp who now lives in Topeka, she remembered as many of the same details about that Halloween party as I had. During our conversation, I shared with her about my thoughts and fears as a little boy without feeling embarrassed. I am now eighty years old and embarrassed by very little, and now, not even scared of the dark anymore.

I still remember this story from seventy-two years ago, and not a Halloween goes by that I do not think of that night in Virgil in 1951. I cross my heart, eyes, legs and swear on two dead cats this is true.

Chapter 30

First Television

Our world changed when we became owners of the latest technology—the television. But my introduction to this extraordinary new device actually occurred in November of 1951.

Just as I and my sister Marilyn were leaving for school, Mamma reminded me again, "Don't get dirty before the bus gets here." The screen door slammed behind us and the dogs came running.

It was a nice day so we waited outside for the school bus to take us to our school in Virgil. I was in the second grade and Marilyn was a sophomore in high school. Happy was trying to jump all over Tubsey, and as always, Old Shep was running about six or seven steps behind. While playing with them, I tried to keep them from jumping up on me as this was a good way to get dirty and I thought of Mamma's warning.

Soon, we heard the old bus come rattling down the gravel road leading to our farm. Marilyn yelled an alert, "Here comes the bus." We had a very large barnyard so the bus simply pulled in and turned around after we boarded. But just before getting on the bus, I looked over at the cow pen and Mickey was looking back at me. I remember thinking what a great horse, and how lucky I was to have her!

Once on the bus, about halfway back I saw my friend and classmate Raymond Engle sitting there with an empty seat beside him. I made my way to him and sat down, happy to be with a friend.

On our way, the bus started its normal rattling and shaking as we traveled down the rough road headed for town. Shortly, we came to the old black iron bridge going over the Verdigris River. The bridge rattled, shook, swayed, moaned, and I was relieved as always when we were over it with a final bump. This occurred every time we crossed the bridge which happened to me thousands of times during my years living near Virgil.

Just as we got off the bridge, it was like a light came on for Raymond as he remembered to share big news. He said, "I heard there are some people in town who have one of those things called a television."

Not knowing what a television was, I asked him what it was. I had never even heard of a television. Raymond told me "it's like a radio with a picture show inside the box."

I was puzzled. "I sure would like to see it. Raymond, do you know where it is?"

Raymond said, "It's supposed to be in the house, just south of the Robinson garage."

Of course I had to see this new contraption, and insisted we go see it as soon as we could.

It wasn't much longer before the bus was pulling into the schoolyard. As we got off, I had more questions. "Have you ever seen one of these things?"

And he surprised me by saying, "No."

We went into our classroom shortly before the bell rang and sat down. The teacher instructed us to practice writing letters of the alphabet. She reminded us that if we forgot how to make them, we could look up above the blackboard where all the letters were displayed with both the capital and lower case. I later realized that probably every first and second grade in the whole country had these same letters displayed in their classrooms.

Since we had both the first and the second grade in one room and only one teacher, she tried to have both classes working on something similar. Soon, I realized maybe the second grade was just a little more advanced in writing alphabet letters because they had more practice.

I was having a hard time with my letters, which was probably because my mind was distracted thinking about that thing called a television. After a while the bell rang and it was recess. Since it was a nice day, everyone went outside and I immediately found Raymond. I told him that since the people who owned the television only lived two blocks down the street, and if we ate our lunch in a hurry, we would have time to get there and back before class started again. Now you have to realize that this was two boys, only six years old, making these plans.

Most of my big ideas resulted in getting either me in trouble or in some predicament, and then needing some help to get out of whatever I had gotten into. But I didn't see how this wouldn't work, even if we were just six-years-old.

I approached Raymond with the idea and he thought it was good, but maybe we should ask the teacher first. I told him I thought that was not a good idea and, besides, the teacher was my sister and it would be okay. I had learned at this early age that if you didn't ask, they couldn't tell you no.

The bell rang and recess was over. We went back inside and continued our studies. I still had a hard time getting my mind on my lessons but finally, the noon dinner bell rang. Raymond and I grabbed our lunches and ran outside. I think it took us less than three minutes to gulp down what we had, and take off north of the school to see the television.

Running all the way, we arrived at the house very fast and became somewhat apprehensive about knocking on the door. Since we had gone all this way, we finally decided there was no turning back. Finally, we went up to the front door and I knocked.

A very nice lady answered the door. I explained why we were there and wanted to see the television. She responded that, at this time of day, it was hard to get any reception, but said she would try. She turned it on and all of a sudden, the screen had some lines going back and forth with noise coming out like the static coming out of our radio at home. Then the screen turned into a constant snowy-looking mess.

She kept saying something about the antenna maybe had to be turned a different direction, but we knew we couldn't wait and had to get back to school. As we were running back, the bell sounded. Shortly after, we made it through the front doors of the school and sat down at our desks. The teacher, Miss Phillips (my sister Frances), said, "You boys look like you've been running a lot."

I simply replied, "Yes, we have." Wow! We made it and never got caught!

I thought television was not as good as the radio. I never saw another one until a couple of years later. The same thing happened—snow and static. I was sure there was no future for television. It was still a while before my family could boast about owning one but, for now, I was okay with that.

I learned later that the people whose house we went to were named Herb and Lois Hart, and that Mr. Hart worked in the oil field. It was known that the oil workers had more money than farmers like us, especially tenant farmers. I learned too that the Kimbells also got a television about the same time as the Harts. The Kimbells were the people whose home I had gone to for the very scary Halloween party, and where Dorothy Kimbell told the story about the wreck on the old black bridge.

Chapter 31 R℗

The Wizard of Oz

We really didn't have many school trips while I attended Virgil, but there is one that stuck with me and will probably never escape my mind. It was in the winter of my first grade 1951, and the teacher was Miss Lewis. She told us we were going to see one of the greatest movies ever. Excitement was running high; we could hardly wait. For this trip, we were going to take the school bus to Eureka. Finally, the day and time came.

Our classes went outside the school where the school bus was waiting for us to load. Oh, how this was going to be fun, going to the movie! It is an understatement that we were all excited and loud. Miss Lewis soon let us know the noise had to stop and it did, kind of.

After getting everyone loaded on the bus, it began to lumber out onto the street turning westward. We were fairly well on our way when we came to the big bridge crossing the Verdigris River. The bus slowed a little and then the front wheels pulled onto the wooden planking of the bridge deck. My how the bridge started to creak, shake, swing and moan! Were we going to make it to the other side? I wondered.

I was afraid this very special treat might turn out to be anything but a treat for me. We were going to see the Wizard of Oz, shown at the Princess Theater in Eureka. The movie had been made in 1939 by MGM theaters, starring Judy Garland, and based on a series of books written in the late part of the nineteenth century by author L. Frank Baum.

To truly understand what this trip meant, I must put everything in prospective. At this time, television had not arrived in Virgil, but changes were coming. I had only seen one movie prior to this one and it was a western shown in the theater in Virgil. I am sure there had been lots of shooting and killing between Indians and cowboys which was typical for the time, but nothing like the Good Witch and Bad Witch. And, there were also those pesky green flying monkeys! It was bad enough that the poor little girl and her dog got blown away and would probably never make it home again. I was petrified and with that came tears.

It is extremely hard to explain how it felt sitting there for such a long time with my legs drawn up to my face, trying not to see or hear anything on the huge movie screen. It just kept going on and on and it was cold in there which didn't help. Today, kids see things like this all the time, even at a much younger age, but for me, I was truly scared. The scariest thing I had experienced prior to this was the coyotes yelping outside our house on the farm, but that was easily overcome by crawling up on my mother's lap and getting a nice warm hug from her.

When the movie was over, we walked out quietly to the bus and boarded without much excitement left in us. The only good thing that happened in the movie was that Dorothy and Toto made it home safely. With our emotions running high, thankfully, it was warm on the bus.

After we boarded, the bus started moving slowly away from Eureka and we were now on our way back to Virgil. Of course, as we approached home, we had to go over that dang old bridge again. Even though I crossed that bridge hundreds of times before I eventually left Virgil, it caused me fear every time I crossed it.

Years later as I was working on this book, I asked a couple of my old fellow Virgil students, Julie (Harris) McKenzie and Carol (Grub) McKenzie, who were older than I, if they had also seen the movie. They both confirmed, "Yes, that is what every class did when the Wizard of Oz came to Eureka." I then asked if they were scared. They both shook their heads together, indicating yes and then Julie said, "I didn't want to see the witch." I felt much relieved I hadn't been the only person who was ever scared by the Wizard of Oz, and that someone else remembered the movie as I had.

To this day, I have never watched the Wizard of Oz completely through, and I probably never will. My kids tease me every time the movie comes on for being so afraid as a young boy.

They try to remind me it is just a movie for the time, a classic.
Even so I can say now, after more than seventy years, that
I no longer wake up fearful of green monkeys or bad witches.

Chapter 32 ℞

Christmas 1951

Since my birthday was just one week prior to Christmas, this meant my mother was going to bring some kind of treat for me and my class. Besides getting something great to eat, my classmates would sing "Happy Birthday" to me. This would happen at the end of the school day. I think the adults in charge thought it would be impossible to get us in the mood to do school work the rest of the day.

Mamma brought cupcakes for everyone, including my teacher Miss Phillips. After school was let out, we looked for Marilyn and both of us rode home with Mamma. When we arrived there, my mother went into the house to start supper preparation.

In class we drew names for Christmas to find out who we were to get a gift for. I was happily surprised and excited that I drew Jill Barry's name. I wanted to buy her a special gift to let her know that I liked her a lot. (There was no way that I wanted to show my affection by kissing like I did with Myrna in the first grade. The teacher even had a talk with us.) I thought this gift might just be the thing though. I told my mother that I had drawn Jill's name and wanted to get her something very special. Mamma did my shopping for me and bought her a beautiful hairbrush and handheld mirror set. I knew this was just perfect. I had such a wonderful mother.

On the last day of school before the start of Christmas vacation, we exchanged gifts. Jill received my gift and seemed to like it very much. Even after this, I wasn't sure she liked me, but I decided to keep trying. We weren't into writing notes to each other or maybe I could have sent her one asking her to mark yes or no, as George Strait did in his 1995 country hit "Mark Yes or No." It seemed that the love life of second graders was very complex with no proper etiquette developed yet. I think on the playground if Jill had tried to chase and catch me, I wouldn't have been smart enough to run slow.

Christmas vacation started on the following Wednesday after my birthday. Christmas was my favorite time of the year for many reasons. I was looking forward to this vacation because I knew both Marilyn and Frances would be home for Christmas. It would be like old times. We could do a lot of different things, but unfortunately, it seemed that both sisters were gone a lot. It turned out to not be as much fun as I had expected. Things were changing. My sisters had a lot more things to do instead of just playing with me. Going on dates and being with friends was now more important.

I still had Christmas to look forward to and Santa Claus would bring me something. I hoped for a saddle and bridle for Mickey, the best horse in the world. My family constantly kept asking if I had really been a good boy. I thought so, but I wasn't really sure I had been good enough.

Finally, Christmas Eve came and I hung my sock on one of the chairs from the kitchen. Mamma asked me if I wanted one of Daddy's and I thought that was a great idea. His feet were bigger so his sock would hold more goodies than mine. Afterwards I crawled into bed, but still had the same question I asked last year: How could Santa come down the pipe and into the potbelly stove?

Morning came and I could hear my mother and father talking in the kitchen. I threw my blanket off, crawled out of bed and started into the kitchen. Before I had gotten two steps, I saw there was a beautiful saddle and bridle on the chair where I had hung Daddy's sock. In addition, there was the usual sock full of candy with a big orange in the toe. There was also a small switch, again!

I immediately picked up the saddle and headed for the door. I was going to show Mickey, but fell down because of its weight. My mother then instructed me to put some clothes and shoes on before going outside because it was cold. Just then, Daddy intervened. "After breakfast we will bring Mickey up to the house and put the new saddle on her." And I agreed.

This had been a wonderful Christmas. The next few days had been a lot of fun riding Mickey with the new saddle, but Mamma was right in that it was cold. I learned in later years that

Mamma and Daddy had ordered a new saddle from Sears and Roebuck, but when it arrived it was too small for Mickey. They then returned that saddle and found a different one locally and purchased it. They were the best parents a young boy could have. Being spoiled has a lot of advantages.

Shortly, a car pulled into our barnyard. As aforementioned, we never had a lot of company so when this happened, I always yelled, "We got company." The car pulled up to the house and it was the county sheriff.

Moving to Yates Center

Monday, December 31, 1951 brought with it news that would change our families' lives drastically. Our landlord Martha Bays gave us a notice, delivered by the Greenwood County Sheriff, to vacate the farm. This notice gave us only sixty days to move—not much time considering what all needed to be done. It wasn't like just finding a new apartment. It almost was like finding yourself a new life.

My family had been on this farm for eight years and I had just turned seven years old two weeks before. My parents did not share family finances with the children and they did not share with me we were going to be moving, although I imagined my parents did share this with my sisters.

The next few weeks, I learned my father and mother seemed to be gone almost all the time during the day while I was in school. I now know they were looking for a new farm and, hopefully, one we could buy.

Daddy started pulling out all the equipment and putting it in rows around the barnyard. He even started laying out things on the hay wagons like old milk cans, old horse harnesses, feed buckets, fence stretchers, and the list went on and on. He even put some of our firewood in the rows. He was getting ready for a farm sale. These sales were considered a major social event, in addition to a time to get rid of all the equipment no longer needed.

There had been a number of these sales around the community for the previous couple of years, and the prices to sell things had been running fairly low. The number of families leaving their farms had been on the increase, and farmers were also purchasing newer and larger equipment as each acquired more acreage for farming.

Finally, my parents could no longer keep from me what was

going on—we were going to move. They purchased a small farm of eighty acres in the Pleasant Grove Township, just about five miles northeast of Yates Center. I don't remember having any real feelings about moving, neither happy or disappointed. I didn't understand what all this meant. I also don't remember discussing this with any of my schoolmates or even with my sisters. I never even wondered what my new school would be like; I was just void of feelings. I only knew this was going to be a big change.

Finally, the Saturday came for the sale and all of my sisters were there along with my two older sisters' husbands. The auctioneer started barking out the bids and then he would say "going once, going twice" and then "sold," and move on to the next item. As I watched our possessions being sold, I think I was sorry most of all to see the new John Deere tractor drive out of the barnyard.

A number of people asked if we were going to sell the paint horse, my Mickey. The answer came back in a resounding, "NO." But they were told that the sorrel mare would be selling soon. I breathed a sigh of relief. I still had my horse and the new saddle which I had just gotten at Christmas time, less than a month earlier.

Many people also came to my parents, telling them they would be missed in the community and wishing them the best on the new farm. There were a lot of hugs. Finally, the sale was over and the place looked empty. Everyone left and it was almost ghostly with not much equipment or many other things left. Daddy had only held back a few chickens, three milk cows and a little baled hay.

What I found out later was that Daddy had already purchased most, if not all, his farm equipment to use on our new farm from the Linn family who lived just up the road to the west of our new place in rural Yates Center. This even included a one-ton truck, a 1946 Ford. A truck was something we had never had before and this truck is still owned by one of the Driskill family members today. Sometime shortly after we got it, I scratched my initials into the hood...RWP. The last time I saw the truck, more than twenty years ago, my initials were still there.

The Linns were part of the migration of farmers who left

the farm after World War II. Emmett Linn took a job working in Wichita, Kansas at the Boeing factory. During the week he worked there, he stayed in Wichita with another local farmer, Herb Wait, who also worked at Boeing. They came back each weekend to Yates Center to be with their families. These were just two of the farmers who left farming permanently. This was one example of how farm life was changing.

Soon, Daddy started taking our remaining possessions over to our new place. Most of this was done by a hay wagon pulled by a tractor. He took the backroads, not having to go through Yates Center. He did have to go over the old black bridge as it swayed, shook, rattled and squeaked. The total distance was approximately twenty miles, which was a long way to ride a tractor in January and February of the year, especially with no winter cover.

I never saw the new place, except on the final trip, and rode with my mother who was driving our car, a 1939 four-door Plymouth with running boards. I don't remember my father tying anything on the car but he teased my sisters that he was going to. They just didn't want to look like people from the dustbowl days. I believe they were called "Okies." At the time, I had no idea what they were talking about.

We were on our way to the new place and stopped in Yates Center to get a few things from the grocery store. This place was much bigger than the Commons' Store in Virgil and had a lot of things. Unfortunately, they didn't have a lady like Mrs. Commons who was kind and caring and had time to help a growing boy, or if they did, I never found her.

From there, we only had about five miles to go. Pulling out on Highway US 54 and traveling about three miles east, then turning on to a gravel road that went north, and going another two miles before we turned east, Mamma said, "Robert, you see that big cedar tree way down there? That is our new place." It was another mile and we were at our new home.

Pulling into the driveway, it was gorgeous. A large row of cedar trees on the north side provided a good wind break, and the house was an attractive two-story with a large front porch. It looked like everything had just received a coat of new white paint.

In the front yard, even though it was winter and the bushes were dormant, you could tell there was a row of approximately fifty peony bushes. Then, in the middle of this row was an arbor on which roses would grow. Mamma seemed to be so excited, and could hardly wait to show me the inside of the house and my own room. Wow! My own room. It was easy to see that the previous owners had really taken care of the property and it was easy to see that the place was going to be simply beautiful when spring came.

We moved into our new house and it was much better than we had in Virgil. It still had an outhouse and no running water, but we did have electricity. And it just felt like this new house was built so much superior to what we had before—the walls were straight and the floors were level. Everything just felt better. It even had a heating stove that ran on propane so we no longer had to cut wood or carry it in. There were lots of windows so it was much brighter inside too.

The one thing we didn't have was a telephone. So, if we needed to get in touch with someone in a hurry, we had to drive to our neighbors, the Weselohs who lived two miles west, down by my new school. In case of an emergency and someone needed to reach us, they would call the neighbor and then the neighbor would come to notify my parents who would then go to their place and return the call. What a mess! But we found everybody there just as friendly as those in Virgil. My Mamma told me country people were just "good people." I have found that basically true throughout all my life. The only problem now is there are not enough of them left.

The morning after our arrival it was Sunday. After getting up and having some oatmeal, it was time for me to go visit the neighbors. Mamma told me they had a young boy just about my age. What I didn't know at the time was that I was on my way to meet and make a very dear friend, Larry Driskill. After seventy years, ours is my longest continuing friendship. We don't get together very often, but we still talk on the telephone now and then. But at least neither of us have to go to the neighbors to make the call. I sometimes reflect how times have changed since today we both carry our phones around with us all the time.

When I finished breakfast, I put my warm winter cap on, and pulled down the ear flaps; put on my coat, mittens, and boots and then headed out the backdoor of the house. I could tell before going outside it was one of those raw winter days. The sky was overcast and drizzling a light rain.

The dogs greeted me and jumped up with their muddy feet before my mother could see it, and then I was quickly off, telling the dogs to stay at home. Once I began my journey, I only had a short distance to go, something like a couple hundred yards before I arrived at the Driskell's place. I think they were our closest neighbor. I remember the rain made the road somewhat muddy as I turned and walked up their driveway, and saw a man and boy working in the yard. They were chopping firewood to take into the house. I remembered how Daddy and I did that back in Virgil. That was some of the first real work I had ever done, and I was so proud when my mother told me how much she appreciated it.

I timidly walked up to the boy with my hands in my pockets, mittens and all. Looking down at the ground, I sheepishly told him that we had just moved in next door and that my name was Robert Phillips. He replied that his named was Larry Driskill and he was glad to meet me. The conversation was started and we talked and talked, and talked some more.

Before long we were exploring his barn, the ravine behind their house, and even their other out-buildings, including their outhouse. In just a short time we were in their house where it was nice and warm, and I met his mother who was the nicest lady you could ever meet. She even gave us a couple of cookies each. Then Larry told me he had seen a paint horse over at our place and wondered if it was mine. I told him that was Mickey and said proudly she was mine. I asked if he would like to go see her, and he replied enthusiastically, "Sure!"

After finishing the cookies and telling Mrs. Driskill thank you, we headed over to our new farm. It was exciting that Larry knew a backway to get to our place. A path went through the ravine, which was overgrown with brush and trees, kind of like going down a jungle path thinking an animal of some kind might jump out at any time. I could see that a lot of vegetation would be growing in the summertime.

Then, about halfway, there was a very small stream which I learned ran part of the time with only a trickle, and other times would run very deep and fast, making it impossible to get through. Exiting from this area it opened up to a trail running next to our apple orchard. It also was somewhat enclosed with a fence on each side. I could see from how the path was worn down, that it had been used a lot. The whole thing was just spooky enough that I knew I would not be using it after dark.

On the way to see Mickey, we ran into my father. We stopped long enough to introduce Larry and then off we went! Mickey was in the corral by the big barn and when she saw us, she nickered and perked up her ears. Then Larry and I went into the barn to get out of the rain and talk about when we might be able to take a ride. I hadn't seen Mickey for a few days so it was great just to go up and give her a big hug around the neck.

Larry and I played, explored and ate a few more cookies before the day was over. I had made a friend. As the years went by, he proved to be very loyal and faithful, one of those individuals you could depend on in the time of need. I am sure our friendship was intensified because of all I had to go through at my young age of seven. I spent a lot of time with Larry and his family during my earlier years and I even lived with them for a while one summer while growing up. As we departed that day and went our separate ways to our homes, I was happy to say to Larry, "See you tomorrow at school."

Life here was so different than in Virgil where my closest friend was a mile away, and, I didn't have a sister at home anymore. Marilyn hadn't moved with us, and Frances was still teaching the first and second grade in Virgil. I could tell already that this move would really change things in my life. But not being able to see the future, I did not know of the other things to come that would turn my whole life upside down. The unknown would affect my life in so many ways with changes that would be more drastic than I could have ever envisioned. Moving was just a minor thing in comparison to what would come.

Chapter 34

Country School

I met Larry on Sunday and now it was time to go to school. It had one room and there were only ten students. Mamma drove me, but on the way, we saw a few kids walking. Once we arrived there, we went inside to meet the teacher Miss Mabel Toadman. She was middle-aged and somewhat of a large woman who told me that there was another second grader and now the class would have two. The total number of students in this school was smaller than the thirteen students we had just in our second grade class in Virgil.

I also found out that since we were a country school, the term would end in mid-April. Sounded good to me...thirty days less than I would have had in Virgil. Thirty days to someone my age was almost like a life time. They said the early dismissal was because the children were needed to help with the spring planting. It was probably an old tradition started a number of years before, and no one ever thought about changing it. I also found that getting out early was allowed by state law for country schools.

The teacher was not very organized and had very little control over the students. I was not used to this and must say I felt very uncomfortable. But, still, the students made me feel right at home. Each day we all brought our sack lunches. It was so great to see what everyone had and to do some trading. I encouraged my mother to always put more in the bag so I would have a lot of trading stock.

The schoolroom had a big chalkboard all across the front of the classroom behind the teacher's desk which sat up on an elevated platform. One of the funniest things that ever happened during the short time I attended this school had to do with the chalkboard and Johnny Weseloh. He got into trouble and Miss Toadman drew a circle on the board and told Johnny to put his nose in the circle and stand there. Johnny, being a creative soul, erased the circle with his noise and then started to move first to the left and then back to the right, all the time with his nose on the blackboard. The thing that made this so funny was Johnny had a runny nose and it left a wet streak, first erasing the circle and then side to side. The teacher's back was to Johnny and she seemed to be oblivious to what was happening behind her. Of course, all the students were having a heyday and laughing while Johnny was pleased to provide the entertainment. I am sure he went home very proud that he had such an opportunity to perform for everyone.

The school building was heated by an old potbelly stove similar to the one we had in our house in Virgil. It was the teacher's job to start the fire each day and make sure it was mostly out after school. The older boys were responsible for adding more wood if needed during the day.

There were two outhouse buildings and they were pretty fancy too. The paper inside was not an old catalog like at home, but the paper was on a roll like what we had at the Virgil school. The doors even closed and there were no cracks in the walls and, besides that, they were even painted! I do think the paint job was a couple of years old as it was a little faded, but I knew someone was trying to make the facilities better. A point not to be overlooked is that each was only a one-hole.

There was even a small barn for you to keep your horse in if you rode it to and from school. You could only imagine what started going through my mind immediately. I could ride to school or, better yet, Larry could ride with me on Mickey. Wouldn't that just be wonderful? I thought.

After our first day at school, the weather was a fairly nice day so everyone walked home. I think I had the farthest to go which was two miles and Larry lived close to our place.

About my riding Mickey to school, my parents weren't much up for the idea. I didn't understand since I had been told by Mamma how she had to ride a horse seven miles to school when she went to Toronto High School. I just didn't understand the difference.

One day, when I wasn't feeling too well or maybe just didn't want to go to school, I stayed at home and then went outside to get Mickey to go for a ride. My father saw me and said that if I was feeling good enough to go riding, I was well enough to go to school. He surprised me by adding, "Why don't you just ride that horse on to school?" I immediately got better. In fact, I suddenly didn't feel bad at all, and off I rode.

Arriving at school on a horse in the middle of the morning caused quite a commotion. When the students saw me ride up, they jumped up and ran outside. Like I said earlier, the teacher had no control. The boys all wanted to help me put Mickey in the barn, and all the girls just wanted to pet her. I was the big man on campus, or maybe I was just the little boy at the country school who had a horse.

The rest of the day was going fairly well until someone looked out the schoolhouse window and saw Mickey going down the road. Seeing that, all of the boys jumped up and the older ones jumped out the windows. Not me, though; I was too little and it was a long way from the window to the ground. Instead, I just went out the front door. We caught Mickey and put her back in the barn, and then went reluctantly back into the school. To my knowledge, not much was learned that day, or as a matter of fact, not much was learned any day. This was a case of the students running the school and doing a poor job of it. The school day finally ended and Larry and I went to get Mickey and rode home without incident.

About a month after being there, the school had a box dinner/supper fundraiser. A lot of detail about this event has been lost to history, but the few high points are as follows: The girls and mothers made a supper and put it in a decorated box which was then laid out on a big table for everyone to see. The men and boys then bid on each box, and whoever made it would share its contents with the buyer. In my case, I wanted to eat with Kathy Linn, my fellow classmate, plus I thought she was kind of pretty. I found out which one was hers, and when the bidding started and her dinner box came up, I was right there to bid. Of course, my father was standing there because he was the one who would be the payer. Before we started the bidding, Daddy said, "Remember now, we aren't buying a horse, so go easy." I then won the bid for a dollar and a half or maybe a little more, but I'm sure it didn't go over two dollars. Most importantly,

I got to eat with Kathy which was a big deal to me as I thought of her as Becky Thatcher from the Tom Sawyer story written by Mark Twain.

Afterwards, it was time to play some games. The only one I remember was that some people were given slips of paper with an item to be cooked, and others were given slips of paper indicating an ingredient. The object was for the person doing the cooking to select ingredients for their preparation. If you selected all the correct items, you were the winner. In my case, I had the slip that had oatmeal on it so I started picking the people who represented the things I needed. First, I knew I had to have oatmeal and then water, but I wasn't sure what else. I can't even remember who any of those people were except that my father also played the game and he represented one teaspoon of salt. Naturally, I wanted to choose him to be on my team, so it was easy to select him. Then someone commented on my choice and said, "He is right but doesn't need a whole teaspoon." Next, someone else spoke up and said, "It all depends on how big the pot of oatmeal is." It was wonderful when I was allowed to be one of the winners with Daddy on my team! I assume they may have bent the rules just a little.

Later we drove home and, on the way, talked about how much fun we had. Now it was just Mamma, Daddy and no sisters. I thought this is the way it will be from now on, and that was okay. I could live with not having sisters at home but I knew they would come home often.

Another memory from my short time attending the country school was the spring fishing outing at the end of the school year. The whole school and a lot of the parents, especially the mothers, went to a big farm pond just about a mile south of the school to fish. Not many fish were caught except for Vic Adams' mother Grace who caught a big bass, and it was really exciting to watch her reel it in. The fish put up a big fight, jumping out of the water a number of times. Eventually she had it on the ground and was able to take the lure out of its mouth. I thought: What a big fish and an exciting catch!

After the day was over, Mrs. Adams went home to clean the fish and then unexpectedly brought it to our house to have for dinner or supper. What a kind thing for a neighbor to do! I wondered if this was just something done to welcome new people.

I actually attended this country school less than sixty days. I do believe the students were happy for school to be out, but I also believe the teacher was happier. My growing up in that community was quite immense but none of it was book-learning.

Chapter 35

R̦

The Baby Calf

I spent almost all my free time with Larry and he was very country-smart, much like Wuwu back in Virgil. One day, as we were going across the pasture, Larry saw a cow having a calf. He told me we would probably need to help the cow. Now we were out of my league, above my pay grade, far beyond my education, and I was very apprehensive.

Larry took a hold of the two front feet that were sticking out and started to pull. He told me to grab a hold and pull too. Not wanting to show my fear of the situation, I did just what he said. Next, out came the head, and then the calf went plop on the ground. Job completed. The mother cow then started licking her baby and soon the calf was standing and suckling milk.

We then went to the house and found Larry's father, telling him what had happened, and that we had done a great job helping the cow to deliver her baby. After all these seventy years since that happened, I have wondered once in a while whether that cow really needed our help, or was it an opportunity for Larry to impress his new friend with how much knowledge he had working with cattle. I was the one who dreamed of being a cowboy, but helping a cow deliver a calf never crossed my mind as cowboy work. I thought it was more about riding my horse and singing, "Back in the saddle again...." with Gene Autry.

I have told a number of my friends that Larry taught me all I ever needed to know in my life by the time I was eight years old. I know this is a great exaggeration, but Larry was really farm and outdoors smart, even if he was only nine years old at the time. He also had an older brother who I am sure taught him a lot more than sisters could teach a little boy. I thought he was lucky to have a big brother, but I loved my sisters and would not have traded them even for two ponies, but don't tempt an eight-year-old boy with four ponies.

Chapter 36   R̖ₚ

Strange Happenings

Soon after I started school at North Pleasant Grove, some unsettling things started happening which would change our family forever.

We hadn't lived long in our new home when my parents again started being gone a lot during the days, almost like when they were looking for a place for us to move. When I went to school, they would leave. One day they told me if I got home and nobody was there, I was to go to the Driskill's place and stay until they got home. Going to the Driskill's was a lot of fun since I got to spend extra time with Larry, and most of the time I ate supper with them. Mrs. Driskill was really a great cook and she made a pie, I think, every day. Of course, her greatest attribute was the love she shared with me and my family.

I guess I really didn't think a lot about why my parents were gone so much. Then one day my father, along with sisters Freda and Frances, stopped at school to pick me up. They said we were going to Emporia as Mamma had been placed in the hospital there. I didn't give it much thought except for thinking that they won't let me in to see her as little kids are not allowed up on the floors where the patients are anyway.

We all went into the hospital and, much to my surprise, they let me go up to Mamma's room. She was lying there, glad to see us all. We visited for a while and then returned to the farm after vowing to be back the next day. I think someone went to see her every day she was in the hospital, and I went most times, if not all. Years later I figured out why they let me go in to see her—she wasn't going to be with us much longer. They knew it, but I didn't.

We visited again a couple more times before the doctors let Mamma come home with Daddy. After Mamma got home, she was up and around a little, but even I knew she wasn't feeling good. I remember going out with her to feed the chickens and I carried the bucket of grain. This was around the end of May, 1952.

Then the day came that I will never forget. The weather was quite nice with the temperatures having been very mild for the past week, and there had been no storms. I spent the day at Larry's place, doing what young farm boys do...exploring. We explored the woods and Cherry Creek which was just east of our place, less than a quarter of a mile away. We could always find something interesting, no matter how many times we went there. Freda had told me not to go very far away just in case she needed to get me. Otherwise, we probably would have been on Mickey riding farther away, maybe even up to see a neighbor like Vic Adams who went to school with us and was just a year or two older than Larry and I.

Two of my sisters, Freda and Frances, had been staying with us to take care of Mamma, and probably to make sure I didn't do anything to get myself into trouble. The neighbors brought prepared food to our place every day, but they didn't stay long. The food was wonderful and the ladies who brought it were very nice. I especially remember Larry's mother Mrs. Driskill; Mrs. Adams, Vic's mother; and Mrs. Wait among many others. Our whole family was treated so nicely with kindness. Like Mamma said, "Country people are wonderful." We had been in the neighborhood for less than four months, but they treated us like lifelong friends.

Then as evening approached, Mamma began to get worse. Freda asked Frances to go to the neighbors and call Lola and Marilyn to come. Daddy had already gone to see if the doctors would come as soon as they could.

It wasn't long before the doctor came and, within the next two hours, both Lola and Marilyn along with their husbands arrived.

I didn't do anything but wander around the house. Freda fixed something for me to eat, but I don't remember being very hungry. I was sitting just outside Mamma and Daddy's bedroom, and could barely hear the doctor and Daddy talking. Then very distinctly, I heard the doctor say to my father, "Bill, she may not live through the night but she could also live a long time." I hung onto that…live a long time…as much as I could.

Freda told me to get ready for bed, which I did and went upstairs to where my room was. Since, in this house I had my own room and not a daybed in the living room, I didn't mind going to bed as much. I must have been really tired as it didn't seem like it took me very long to go to sleep.

The next thing I knew, my sister Freda came upstairs and woke me and said, "Robert, Mamma has gone to be with Jesus." I did not shed a tear because my mother had told me at Grandma Young's funeral about a year earlier that "big boys don't cry." I was going to honor her and be brave and grown up.

I got up and went downstairs but never looked into Mamma's room. Then I went outside. Larry soon came over and told me he had heard about my mother. We just walked around talking about what, I do not recall, just talking. I had no idea what my sisters or my father were doing. I was just numb and, in a daze, not feeling anything.

No one ever told me my mother was going to die. I wouldn't have known how to say goodbye so I guess that was best. I knew that I had a strong family around me and that we would go on. What I didn't know was how much I would miss those hugs and being told everything will be all right, especially when the coyotes yelped and I was really scared. Looking back, as a young boy I really missed my mother, and I still miss her to this day.

She went to be with Jesus on June 7, 1952. After her death, over a number of years, I learned many things about my mother's illness. As we were moving, Mamma started feeling bad, and once the move to Yates Center was done, Daddy and she started visiting a number of doctors. Finally, after a visit to Dr. Pees of Iola, Kansas (only about 20 miles from our home on the new farm), he diagnosed her with cancer.

She was then admitted to the Newman Hospital in Emporia. There they did exploratory surgery and found she was completely full of cancer. That is when she came home to live out the very few days she had left.

My sister Frances told me years later that Mamma had noticed lumps in her breast but did not know what to do, and did not tell anyone. Frances also told me that as our mother approached the end, she was afraid that I would grow up and not remember her. This, of course, has not happened. I think of her every day, and especially honor her wish by not letting anyone ever call me "Bob," which was her concern when naming me Robert.

After moving to Lawrence, I found my own personal physician and it was Dr. Gerald Pees, the son of the doctor who had diagnosed cancer in my mother. What a really small world. This was as unlikely as finding someone from Virgil, but it does happen.

Chapter 37

R
P

The Last Goodbye

This was probably the saddest day of my life. It was Tuesday, June 10, 1952 only three days after my Mamma passed away. It was just long enough after Mamma's death that reality finally sunk in. It was the day for the final goodbye, her funeral. We gathered at the Methodist Church in Virgil where Mamma was a member and had attended since she, Daddy, Freda and Lola had moved to the Virgil area in October 1929. The little church was built in 1879 and had begun earlier at the home of F.G. Allis, about a mile south of what finally become Virgil.

As we all gathered, there was a dark cloud of sadness hanging over us, even though it was a very nice and beautiful day with the sun shining brightly, and the birds flying high and singing their joyous songs. Mamma would have loved this day—a great day to work in the garden or to attend to the chickens. She was always busy preparing for her family and seemed to love every moment of it.

I knew we were really going to miss Mamma, although I really hadn't grasped the magnitude of what this all meant. I would never have her there again to comfort me if I were sad or afraid; she wouldn't be there to meet my wife or to hold my children. This was a lot for me as a seven-year-old to grasp and even to cope with, but I knew that I had my Daddy and four loving sisters. Little did I know how much those sisters would mean to me over the coming years.

When we gathered at the quaint, small white church sitting on the hill across from the Virgil School, everyone was very quiet. There were lots of hugs and people saying how sorry they were for our loss, and what a wonderful person our mother was.

Everyone went inside, walking past the casket where Mamma was lying. I hardly looked that way because the pain was so great. I walked in with Daddy and sat by him. Freda was sitting on my right side and put her arm around me to give me a little hug. My other sisters were to her right. The preacher, Rev. William Zimmerman, gave the sermon, followed by the songs "Good Night" and "Good Morning" plus "Garden of Prayer" sung by Willard Shaw, and then a poem which had been written by Alberta Ireland, a family friend:

In Memory of Mabel Phillips

Today our hearts are almost breaking and our eyes with tears o'er flow, For the one we loved so dearly, has gone the way we all must go.

We shall sadly miss her presence, but we are glad her suffering is over, for in that bright home in heaven pain and sickness come no more.

She was such a good companion. Loving mother and true friend, and she trusted in her Savior who was with her to the end.

Up there in that fair city, when our own life's day is over. We shall meet again our loved one and be parted never more.

The pallbearers were: Henry Hanson, D. Commons, Harvey Aeschilman, William Storrer, D. B. Burris and Lon Reams.

When the service was over, the preacher had everyone walk by the open casket, and when everyone was gone except the family, the reverend said a few words to us and then a prayer. After that, our family again walked by Mamma lying in the casket. Again, I did not shed one tear, but my sadness really hurt. The only reason I was able to not shed tears was a tremendous desire to honor my Mamma.

After everything was over, everybody went outside the church and just stood around—again with lots of visiting, hugs and tears. I must have gotten patted on my head a million times and I overheard a lady saying, "What a sad thing for that little boy." She was very right.

I guess it was the funeral director Mr. Campbell who, after visiting with Daddy, got the pallbearers together to load the casket in the hearse. People just stood very quietly with heads bowed as the casket was carried by. After it was loaded into the hearse, everyone went to their respective cars in order to form a procession to the Yates Center Cemetery. Daddy, my four sisters, and I were loaded into a very big black car for the trip.

We traveled very slowly through downtown Virgil, passing almost all of the businesses, and not much faster on the gravel road in route to the cemetery on the north side of Yates Center. The procession went around and through the many sections of graves following the road, and finally came to a halt on the northeast side of the cemetery.

Everyone finally got out of their cars and walked to a place where a few chairs and a tent had been set up. Mr. Campbell came over to us and asked us to follow him. We then walked to the chairs, and I sat down beside Daddy and Freda, with my other sisters on the same front row.

People gathered around while Reverend Zimmerman said a few words and then a prayer. I sat there with tears almost flowing but I remembered again that Mamma said, "big boys don't cry," and I didn't.

Afterwards, people started visiting, but it wasn't long before everyone left. Daddy, Frances and I went back to our new farm east of Yates Center. My other sisters and their husbands went their respective ways.

Chapter 38

Summer 1952

After the funeral, I lived that summer on the farm with my sister Frances and my father. I spent a lot of time riding Mickey, petting the dogs, and playing and exploring with Larry. It wasn't long before Larry and I had almost become brothers. He never pulled tricks on me like my sisters had, but we did get into small disagreements now and then.

I remember one day Larry and I got into a fight, over what I don't recall, but his father saw what was going on. He stopped the fight and whipped Larry, but left me unpunished. I went home but within thirty minutes, Larry and I were back playing with each other. Larry soon took his pants down and we counted the whip marks on his legs. I felt really badly for him, but not so bad that I volunteered for a whipping myself.

Life was a little different after Mamma passed. On one occasion, Daddy was running short of hay so he and I made a trip to Des Moines, Iowa. Strangely, we really didn't look for any hay and, of course, came back without any. I really believe the trip was just for him to see his sister and brother who lived there.

His sister Edna was a very religious person and believed the Lord had chosen her to live forever. She once had cataracts on her eyes and had lost vision for a number of years, and when cataract surgery became available, they were removed. She could see again and, from that point on, she was really even more convinced she was not going to die—the Lord had given her sight again so He must want her to live. Her theory was disproven when she died a few years later.

I especially remember an event that summer when the neighborhood had a big ice cream social in our barnyard during July. It seemed like hundreds of people came, but I'm sure there weren't that many. My father and Herb Wait, a neighbor, began an ice cream eating contest. Herb cheated by dumping some of his ice cream out in the bush behind where he was sitting. I was told later by Larry that Herb was kind of ornery that way. I don't remember who won and it didn't really matter. I just remember never seeing so many ice cream makers in one place, and I haven't seen that many since.

The ice cream social was just a great neighborhood celebration. I don't know who organized it, but I am sure it was to make us feel welcome in the neighborhood, and to help us get over our sorrow. I was very grateful for that.

That summer I grew up a lot. I think the main thing that kept me going was the love from my sister Frances, my father, and my friendship with Larry and his parents.

Chapter 39

Returning to Virgil

The summer was coming to an end and the question was what to do with me. My father did not feel comfortable with me remaining on the farm and continuing to attend the country school, and now there were no sisters living at home. Since Frances was returning to Virgil to continue teaching the first and second grade, a family meeting took place around the first of August about what to do with me.

It was determined that when school started in the fall of 1952, I would return to Virgil for the third grade. My life had changed drastically from what it had been the prior year when I started second grade in Virgil. It was a very beneficial decision as I was back among classmates whom I knew, and it made me feel extremely welcome. My sister Frances was still teaching the second grade there, but I was no longer in her class.

I am sure my fellow classmates knew very little of what I had been through, and probably would not have understood what I had experienced the previous six months. How could they? I was struggling with everything that had transpired myself.

One of the stabilizing factors that helped me that year was having Miss Mamie C. Allis as my teacher. She had been around Virgil for a long time, born there on February 17, 1890. She had also been an elementary school teacher for 41 years with 35 of those in the Virgil School. The other stabilizing factor was that my sister Frances was teaching just across the hall.

I was now living on oil leased land about five miles east of Virgil with my sister Marilyn and her husband Dale Sauder, along with their new baby Sheila. The house was very small and in poor condition, but you had to do with what you had, and we did. It's strange to think that just twelve months earlier, I was riding the school bus with Marilyn and now she was taking care of me, acting kind of as my mother.

I was now riding the bus by myself. It was especially a big change for me with no longer having my dogs to meet me each day when I was dropped off at home. Things just weren't the same—no Mamma to give me a hug, or Mickey to go and see and possibly go for a ride.

To put things into perspective, my sister was only sixteen years old, her husband Dale was just seventeen about to turn eighteen, and their daughter Sheila was only five months. The stress on both of them must have been tremendous, both financially and emotionally. I did find myself sometimes with tears running down my cheeks for what seemed no reason. I now assume this was depression, but a boy of seven years just didn't understand such things, or at least I didn't. All I knew was that big boys don't cry, and I wanted to be really grownup and make my mother proud.

I was sad because I didn't have friends there to ride the bus with me like I had living across the river on the Bay's place—like Raymond Engle, Ronni Christlieb, Carl Jones and their brothers and sisters. Again, I learned the hard lesson that you don't know how good it is until you don't have it. Even a sister on the bus with me, sitting on the other side, gave me a good feeling—kind of a safety net.

It was about the first of November when a family meeting was held again, without me, and it was decided I should move to Toronto and live with my oldest sister Freda and her family. That included husband Floyd Wayne Gibson, and their four-year-old daughter Judy. I continued to go to Virgil for school, but instead of the bus, I rode back and forth with the school music teacher Miss Harder who also lived in Toronto. I did this until third grade was over in May of 1953.

I liked Miss Harder a lot; she was very nice and easy to talk with. Some days she would have to stay a little late and I just hung out around the front steps of school. Then one day, an older boy came up to me and explained that he had lost his new wristwatch. The clock part had come off his wristband and he asked if I would help him look for it. He said if I happened to find it, he would give me a dollar, and he went on to explain that he had lost it going from the schoolhouse to the gymnasium.

Having nothing else to do, and knowing I could use a little

money, I walked back and forth a number of times over the path the boy had traveled, and there it was. There was a place by the school where you had to jump down, and maybe the jar of landing caused the watch to come off. I really wish I had remembered his name, but the dollar I will remember forever. Back then it was a lot of money, and for an eight-year-old, it was huge.

Christmas 1952

I t was Tuesday, December 18, 1951 and only one week from Christmas and my birthday. School let out at noon and, instead of riding with Miss Harder back to Toronto where I had been staying since the previous month, I went with my sister Frances to Yates Center to be with Daddy. That birthday was my first without Mamma, and it would be the first Christmas too. I was excited to see Daddy, ride Mickey, and also see Larry Driskill.

Frances and I left Virgil headed for the new farm and traveled on the gravel road to the east. This seemed to me to be the longest straight road in Kansas, which later I found was not the case, but it still was a long road. We took highway US 75, then US 54, and finally turned down country roads to soon be at the farm in Yates Center. Daddy was there waiting and extremely glad to see us, and we were happy to see him as well. Before we went into the house, my two wonderful dogs, Happy and Tubsey, ran to me excitedly wagging their tails and jumping on me, wanting to be petted. Since it was a really nice day, I went to see Mickey before going into the house.

That evening, Frances fixed our supper of meatloaf from things she found in the refrigerator and cupboards. Over the years, Frances became famous for her meatloaf with all the unusual ingredients she put into it like mashed potatoes, Cheetos, corn and anything else she found edible. And don't forget my favorite...a lot of ketchup! We ate supper and started visiting; it just felt really good being together again and talking for what seemed hours. Frances also found what was needed to bake a birthday cake for me. I remember that it was a flat cake with white icing and eight candles.

Since we were there for Christmas, the conversation turned to a Christmas tree. Daddy reminded us that when our family first moved in, a lone cedar tree was standing by a fence row just southeast of the house and Mamma said, "that tree will be for next Christmas." So, it was settled that the tree had been chosen and, in a small way, it felt like Mamma was still with us.

Over the next three or four days, Frances did some house cleaning, laundry for Daddy, and shopping to get ready for the rest of the family to arrive for Christmas. I spent a lot of time being with Larry and riding Mickey when it wasn't too cold. Mrs. Driskill said she was glad to see me, which made me feel really good.

Soon, Christmas Eve arrived along with my other sisters and their families which included my two nieces: Judy now about five years of age and Sheila still a baby. Daddy and I went to cut down the tree and then brought it back to the house. It was very big and needed a lot of trimming to finally fit into the living room. Frances and Marilyn decorated it with lights and other ornaments we brought from Virgil. Afterwards, we had our Christmas Eve dinner which was only sandwiches made from things bought at the grocery store just a couple of days prior. Daddy hadn't been much of a cook and had started eating most of his evening meals with the Driskills. We could tell Daddy was extremely lonely living there by himself.

Freda helped me with a chair to hang one of my father's socks on it in case Santa knew where I was. Luckily, he did find me and there was not only a sock full of candy with a big orange in the toe, but a pair of the most beautiful cowboy boots too—black with red and white designs in the upper part of the boot. I loved those boots so much I even slept with them on for a few days before getting some horse manure on them.

After dinner on Christmas, everyone left for their homes except for Frances and me. We stayed a couple more days before she took me to Toronto to be with Freda, and then she went back to Virgil.

Chapter 41

The Picnic

School was a blur that year but the last day of the term was the class picnic. It was so much fun and I enjoyed it so much that I still remember it vividly today. In fact, I recall there was great anticipation by everyone.

Miss Harder came by my sister's house in Toronto and picked me up for the last trip to Virgil. Freda had packed a larger sack lunch for me as our class was going on a picnic to celebrate our last day of third grade and the last day of school. What a year I had—living with one sister and ending up living with another, but still spending the whole year in Virgil grade school.

The weather was simply fantastic. The sun was shining super bright with not a cloud in the sky and the temperature was as close to perfect as it could be—not hot and not cold—just right for an outdoor outing. Miss Harder drove through downtown Toronto and soon turned onto Kansas State Highway 7 going to US Highway 54. There we turned west for a couple miles before turning on a road marked Virgil, then down the country roads the rest of the way. It was spring and the birds and baby rabbits were out in large numbers, along with the bugs which would go splat on the windshield now and then. We had the windows rolled down and a soft breeze with a little dust kept blowing in.

Before long we were going through Quincy and then on the way to Virgil, crossing the Verdigris River. When we pulled up to the school, the buses were just letting students off and I yelled to Carl Jones and Ronnie Christlieb. Everyone went inside and we took our places at our desks. You could just feel the excitement in the air with everyone talking loudly. Miss Alice tried to keep some order but she was having a hard time, or maybe she wasn't trying very hard. That day, we didn't really have any lessons, but just told each other what we were going to do that summer. I guess it hadn't hit me yet that I would not be returning to the fourth grade in Virgil; I had very little to say about that and my summer would be in Toronto living with my sister.

Finally, it was lunchtime when Miss Alice got our attention and told us it was time to go. She instructed us to get into two lines as we were going to a surprise place and needed to follow her. Everyone wanted to know where this place was and she kept saying "just follow me." We continued with our two lines in front of the school and headed north past the Methodist Church where my mother's funeral had been held less than twelve months earlier. We only went one block north and turned east one block and now were on Main Street.

Proceeding north past the EUB (Evangelical United Brethren) Church, we soon came to the Commons' Store where Mrs. Commons was standing at the front door saying hello to all of us as we went by. Mrs. Commons was known as a very friendly, caring and patient person. Maybe she could have been considered the community "mother" because of her concern and caring for all of the children who lived in and around Virgil, and I was especially one of those.

I knew we were making quite a bit of noise, but no one seemed to mind. The boys were doing what boys do—teasing each other with some friendly pushing as we traveled along, with the girls joining in, in some cases. We were just having fun and not a care in the world.

Soon we were in front of Kussman Soda and then on to Pennebaker's Grocery Store where Frank Pennebaker was standing outside watching us all pass by. Someone yelled, "Myrna, there's your father," and she looked up and waved to him as we continued on. We still did not know where we were going but Miss Alice led us across another street in front of residential houses. The first one I recognized was the Kimbell house where I had gone to that very scary Halloween party, and then a little farther past Margret Berry's house. "Where are we going?" we asked again. We thought maybe out in the country somewhere.

Then we came to the very large stone house that the Dalton's built in the 1870s on the west side of the road. We were then definitely in the country and coming to a fork in the road where we had to go east or west.

We turned right and, after going only about a hundred yards, turned right again into a very nice large meadow. Miss Alice announced, "We are here." It was almost on top of the hill so looking somewhat northwest, I was able to see the place where we once lived. It made me a little sad, but there was no time for that—this was going to be fun.

We seemed to break up in a few groups, mostly boys in one and the girls in another. Miss Alice said we could take out our picnic lunches and after that, we would play some games. We sat there laughing and enjoying ourselves until then. Once in a while, a car or truck drove by and we waved and the drivers honked their horns. This was fun!

There were many birds there that day. Barn swallows flew just above the grass to catch bugs, diving and swooping around like dive bombers, and then we heard a quail saying, "bob, bob-white" and again "bob, bob-white." There was also a meadow lark sitting on the fence post by the road, and we could see a number of crows flying over to the south toward town and hear them saying their infamous, "caw, caw, caw." They flew a short distance and landed in the tree tops. Then someone found a box turtle which caused a great commotion when the person who picked it up got their hand peed on.

It eventually came time for the games. They were all of the kind that involved a lot of running, like drop the handkerchief. And finally, it was time to return to school. Miss Alice put us back into our lines and off we went, returning the same way we had taken to our destination. We continued laughing and having a good time but with less energy.

Once back at the school, we went inside to our room and, for the last time, sat down at our desks. Miss Alice gave us a short talk, telling us how much she enjoyed having us as students and how she was looking forward to the third graders being back next year as fourth graders. Everybody ran off very fast as if the school house were on fire. I went out into the hall and saw my sister, Miss Phillips, bidding farewell to her first and second graders. She told me she would be over to Toronto to pick me up the next day so we could go see Daddy and the new farm.

It had been one of those sad days in saying goodbye, but also a happy day too. What I didn't know was that the real sadness was that I would most likely never see any of those students ever again.

I got in the car with Miss Harder for the trip back to my sister's place in Toronto. We were both fairly quiet; I was thinking about getting to see my father the next day. When we arrived at my sister's house, I got out and told Miss Harder, "Thank you." She drove off and I never saw her again either.

Postscript

All books have to come to an end, although it is hard to stop writing and say, "It's finished." This book was no exception, especially when there is so much more to impart than I anticipated. When the book started to look like the size of *Gone with the Wind*, something had to be done. The solution was simply to publish two books instead of one.

This memoir is to be followed by the history of the community where I grew up titled, *The Birth and Demise of a Small Flint Hills Town*. The second book creates a duology to hopefully be published later this year.

The new book will encompass the lives of settlers who arrived in Kansas for the inexpensive or free farmland made available after the Civil War. Soon after their arrival, a post office and churches were established along with medical doctors setting up their practices. Then came the railroad, a hotel, the Mafia (yes, The Mafia), and a newspaper in conjunction with oil production and the establishment of an exceptional school system which produced superior athletes. Included is personal history remembered by many former residents of Virgil, Kansas and its surrounding area, a once thriving community that eventually saw decline to become a virtual ghost town.

On the next page is our third-grade class photo taken in the spring of 1953. I am so pleased to have found this picture in my sister's belongings after her death. The photo was one of the big motivators for me to write this book.

Back row: Myrna Pennebaker, Wilma Drake, Luvena Nibarger, Margaret Berry and Jill Berry.

Front row: Raymond Engle, Robert Phillips, Troy Crabtree, Carl Jones, Ronnie Christlieb and Carl Smith.

(Insert photo of class with the caption. Taken in spring of 1953.)

To date I have found the following classmates and visited by phone with four of them: Margaret (Berry) Culp, Ronald Christlieb, Myrna (Pennebaker) Chambers and Carl Jones. I have

THIRD GRADE—Back row—Myrna Pennebaker, Wilma Drake, Luvena Nibarger, Margaret Berry, and Jill Berry.
Front row—Raymond Engle, Robert Phillips, Troy Crabtree, Carl Jones, Ronnie Christlieb, and Carl Smith.

Robert and classmates, third grade, Virgil, 1953.

especially been very fortunate to make contact with Carl. My wife and I had a wonderful time getting together with him and his wife Janann, and visiting for hours. We both had been living in Lawrence for over twenty years, but did not realize it and just got together a few days ago.

Those classmates assumed deceased: Jill Berry, Luvena Nibarger, Raymond Engle, Troy Crabtree, and Carl Smith. The only one I do not know the status of is Wilma Drake.

I hope you have enjoyed reading *Big Boys Don't Cry* and I hope you read my next book, *The Birth and Demise of a Small Flint Hills Town,* A History of Virgil, Kansas.

A special note about Larry Driskill. I was very fortunate to have two wonderful visitors to our home just as I was working on my final chapters of this memoir—Larry and Karen Driskill. I hadn't seen them for about ten years. They had just returned to the mainland from Alaska where they had lived for a number of years, and now only spend the summer months there. Since I had been working on this project for over two years, and Larry was a very important part of my life, I gave them what I had written and asked for their feedback. Larry told me I was pretty much on track with everything, except I hadn't mentioned the great amount of pain my mother was in at the end of her life. I asked him to explain. Larry told me that my mother was so much in pain that they could hear her moaning and crying at night, all the way to their home. He said, "My family felt so bad for her; we just wanted to "cry." This came across to me as very powerful and sad, and at that moment my heart ached.

The distance from house to house was approximately one hundred and twenty yards, just across the small branch of the Cherry Creek that separated our places. At night we did not have any traffic going by our homes—no cars or trains, and no airplanes flying over. It was just country-quiet. The only sounds at night coming from the outside were maybe a frog croaking and bugs chirping, or possibly a coyote now and then. Mamma's moans and crying obviously carried quite a distance in this environment. It was also late spring and everyone slept with the windows opened to get the maximum amount of air through the rooms. Larry even said that, while his family sat on the porch swing, they could hear my mother moaning and crying.

But why didn't I have any memory of hearing these moans and cries of pain? My room was separated from Mamma and Daddy's room by a number of walls and was on the other side of the house. I think youngsters sleep a little sounder than grownups and I would have been very tired from just spending all my time outside being a very active seven-year-old, or maybe I just blocked it out of my mind. This revelation of my mother's pain, described by Larry, stunned me so much that it put me into a state of sadness. How I wish I would have known what to do to help make my mother more comfortable! This sadness still lives inside of me seventy-two years later. I keep remembering how much I loved my mother and always wanted to do things to make her proud and happy. But, in this case, I feel I let her down, even though I didn't know the severity of her circumstance and that she was going to die.

I cannot grasp the grief my father must have been experiencing, at that time, trying to take care of my mother and me. He did have help from my sisters. Frances moved in with us as soon as the schoolyear was over in Virgil, and Freda and her daughter Judy spent a lot of time with us also. I know he was very appreciative.

Acknowledgements

There is no way this endeavor could have been completed without the help and encouragement of many people. First, I want to thank my wife Beverly for her patience, as this has been a long and tedious undertaking, spanning almost three years. She became my number one proofreader and critic, and due to my inability to drive, Beverly has also been my main chauffeur, transporting me all over the eastern part of Kansas. We have made trips to Topeka, Virgil, Eureka, Emporia, El Dorado, Olpe, Yates Center, and other small towns in Kansas.

Maureen Carroll, Editor-in-Chief of Anamcara Press, President of Kansas Authors Club, District Two. She referred Vicki Julian to be our editor and has been most helpful in making this book a reality.

Vicki Julian, my editor. As it turned out, I helped Vicki and her husband Steve in building their house over forty years ago, and we had lost contact until I needed an editor and book publishing expert. She worked closely with Beverly and me, offering not only editing services, but general publishing guidance and help in finding publishing services.

My son Andrew was a great supporter who also provided transportation to accomplish tasks such as document copying, etc.

My daughter Lei Anh Phillips Russell, who lives in Pace, Florida, kept encouraging me and always asked, "Daddy, how is the book coming?"

My granddaughter Stella Williams, working with her grandmother Beverly, assisted in transposing almost unreadable newspaper clippings from the 1800s so they could be read and used as part of this story.

Ginger Williams, stepdaughter, IT advisor and supporter

Adam Williams and Benji Russell, my two sons-in-law

Grandchildren: Blake Russell, Myles Phillips, Cole Phillips, Stella and Sienna Williams

Dawn Claus, blind rehab specialist, VA Hospital, Leavenworth, Kansas

Maureen Frances, blind rehab specialist, Hines VA Hospital, Chicago, II.

Linda (Aeschliman) Snyder, Virgil school alumna

Lucille (Aeschliman) Barb

Charles Williams, a blind veteran who I met while attending the Blind Rehab Center in Birmingham, Alabama, assisted in helping me locate telephone numbers on his smart phone. He also kept encouraging me each time we talked by phone, which was weekly.

Encouragement also came from my Vietnam vet's support group out of the Leavenworth VA hospital and led by Jesse Thomas, and members Henry Paustian, Ken Ballard, Eddie Peele and Ronald Baily.

Ann Vigola Anderson, the first author I talked to about writing this book. She had published *Posts of a Mid-Century Kid* with Anamcara Press and encouraged me to get started.

Shawn Wangerin, photographer, Essence of Nature Photography

John Bills, researcher, Greenwood County Historical Society

Joyce Bills, researcher, Greenwood County Historical Society

Sam Robison, Virgil Historian

Robin Himes, Executive Director, Greenwood County Historical Society

Sheryl Moody, staff member, Greenwood County Historical Society

Judy Lawrence, my niece

Larry and Karen Driskill, content advisors and friends

Gary Bowman, Virgil historian

Dick Albert, special historian of Virgil

Janice (Hawkins) Casey

Pete Watts, Virgil oil production specialist

John and Orella Hosack, Virgil history specialist

Carol (Grub) McKenzie

Julie (Harris) McKenzie

Ron Storrer, Virgil historian

Margret (Barry) Culp, Virgil classmate 1950-53

Dwayne "Doc" Scott, medical advisor for the time period of 1940-55.

Sam Milner, content advisor for High School All-State father Jerry Milner

Carl Jones, Virgil classmate 1950-53

Maggie Witte, CKLS Talking Book Service, Emporia, Kansas

Denis Hill, former Virgil resident and author

Alan and Bobbie Jaax, content advisors and friends

Hugh and Linda Nicks, content advisors and friends

Gus, Virgil ambassador and "president" of the Virgil welcoming committee, also known as the town dog

About the Author

Robert W. Phillips was born in Eureka, Kansas located in the great Flint Hills where he spent most of his formative years. As a young child on afarm near Virgil, he acquired the values that have influenced him throughout his life. As his mother always said, "Country people are good people."

After graduating from Maize High School, he attended Kansas State University and Kentucky University, finally earning his degree from Wichita State in 1969. He also received a commission as a Second Lieutenant from ROTC and spent three years in the military, including a tour in Viet Nam.

After retiring from a successful career in business, writing became his passion. It provided him with a way to keep his mind active and allowed his creative skills to run rampant. He currently lives in Lawrence, Kansas with his wife Beverly and a cat named Simon.

I hope you enjoyed reading my story,
"BIG BOYS DON'T CRY."
Please order additional copies from your favorite
bookseller and leave a review for me on
their website!

www.ingramcontent.com/pod-product-compliance
Lightning Source LLC
Chambersburg PA
CBHW060145130626
46556CB00006B/2506